HOME

Noni Hazlehurst's

HOME

with
Susan Dalton and Robert Francis
and expert advice from Jackie Warren Dip Art (Int Des)

HODDER

A Hodder Book

Published in Australia and New Zealand in 2000
by Hodder Headline Australia Pty Limited
(A member of the Hodder Headline Group)
Level 22, 201 Kent Street, Sydney NSW 2000
Website: www.hha.com.au

NATIONAL LIBRARY OF AUSTRALIA CATALOGUING-IN-PUBLICATION DATA

Hazlehurst, Noni
Noni Hazlehurst's home.

ISBN 0 7336 1290 3

1. Interior decoration. 2. Home economics. I. Title.

645.

Designed by Liz Seymour, Seymour Design
Photographs of Noni Hazlehurst by Jennifer Soo
Photographs of homes and interiors courtesy of McGrath Partners
Printed by APG, Maryborough

Contents

Introduction

When I started hosting the Seven Network's 'Better Homes & Gardens' in 1994, I made it clear to the producers that I wasn't going to pretend to be an expert. Like many people who watch the show, I don't have a lot of confidence in my ability to put together a 'look' or to choose the right colour. My taste has always been what you might call 'eclectic', which is a fancy way of saying a hodge-podge of colours, objects, finishes and styles.

But I've learnt a lot over the years, picking up tips from the real experts who work on the program and for the magazine and, while making choices is still difficult, at least I'm prepared to try. I'm more likely now to be a bit adventurous and less likely to slavishly copy someone else's style, whether it suits me or not.

I've come to accept that I really only have to suit myself and that it's OK for my home to be a reflection of me and my family — where we've been, what we've done and what we hold dear. If no one else likes it, it doesn't matter.

My home will always be a work in progress. It will never be finished because as I grow I change, and so do my tastes. And as my children develop and change, so do the family's needs and priorities.

Above all else, I like my home to be casual and relaxing. I don't want it to look like the stylised photos that you see in design books and expensive magazines, where three casually strewn lemons and a light sprinkling of coffee beans adorn the coffee table, or there are so many fancy cushions and throw rugs on the couch that there's no room for bottoms.

The idea behind this book is to give you as much knowledge of the available options as possible, so you can make an informed choice. At least if you know what to expect when you visit a showroom or hardware store, you won't be totally overwhelmed by the plethora of possibilities.

Too many choices make decisions difficult, and I'm not ashamed to admit that I've been known to back out of tiling shops, for example, too confused to order anything other than plain cream tiles with a bit of a border. And faced with three million paint colours, with unhelpful names like Tango Sauce or Whyalla Sky, I've thrown my hands up in despair and painted everything white.

If you don't know what you're after it's easy to be influenced by a salesperson who, with possibly the best intentions, doesn't really know you or your home. Mistakes can be very costly.

You need to work out how you use your home — how it functions or how you'd like it to function. When you've made these fundamental decisions, you can narrow down your range of options considerably.

Your budget will obviously affect your choices and so will those things in your home that you can't or don't want to change — furnishings, fittings, precious objects or pieces of furniture and so on.

Whatever you do, don't be persuaded into thinking that style is something you have to learn or buy. If your home or parts of it and the way you live in it suits you, then you already have style — your own.

There are no perfect solutions when it comes to making a house a home, so forget about getting it right — take your time, do your homework and try to enjoy the process.

Floors

STARTING FROM THE GROUND UP

THE POOR OLD FLOOR, it cops the lot. It gets walked on day and night with high heels and football boots. It gets danced on, pots and pans get dropped on it, it suffers baby's and puppy dog's 'accidents' and the crumbs and spillages of over-indulgent dinner parties. It bears the brunt of whole families growing up; soaks up ink and ballpoint pen stains, modelling glue and paints. Floors take more punishment than any other part of the house, so your choices need to take this into consideration. And it's important to get floors right the first time, because changing them is a major hassle.

Some friends of ours have a 'no-shoes inside' rule — even for visitors (and I must say, their timber floors have lasted a lot longer than mine.) My great aunt, who lived in Canada, made people wear plastic bags, secured with rubber bands, over their socks, which I thought was really going too far. A boot scraper at the front door is a good investment but, whatever you do, floors are going to take a beating and will need constant attention to keep then looking good.

Carpets: wool, nylons, acrylics, other man-made materials ➢ runners ➢ rugs ➢ sisal, coir and seagrass ➢ polished timber ➢ oiled timber ➢ painted and varnished timber ➢ timber patterns ➢ parquet ➢ cork ➢ vinyl and linoleum ➢ rubber ➢ tiles: vinyl, rubber, ceramic ➢ terracotta ➢ slate ➢ quartzite ➢ marble ➢ terrazzo ➢ granite ➢ concrete ➢ brick

In the beginning there was the floor. The only material our early ancestors had to choose from for the floors in their simple dwellings was from the earth around them — the earth on which the house was built, sometimes mud baked hard by the sun, or dried woven reeds and grasses. Our arctic ancestors used skins on the floors of their icy dwellings, the Egyptians and the Romans used stone, fired tiles and slate, while the tribes of tropical Indonesia and Melanesia built timber floors for their longhouses suspended high in the rainforests.

When you think about it, the modern floor is not vastly different in principle from the ancient floor. Of course, earth floors are few and far between these days, especially in wealthier countries. Flooring timber is now tongue and groove, and comes in many different styles and colours, and concrete and vinyl are the big new inventions, but the basic materials — wood, stone and terracotta — are still very popular just as they were in Roman times. The evolution has been not so much in the materials available but in the technologies available for manufacture and in the gradual development of design and decoration country by country, culture by culture.

Over the last century the North American home has featured a vast array of timbered floors both in hardwoods and softwoods — maple, hickory, oak, ash, walnut, yellow pine and white pine. In Scandinavian countries the timber, bleached or decorated with geometric designs, gave way to parquet and pale timber blocks, while in Mediterranean Europe terracotta tiles have continued to reign supreme. In England, the fitted or wall-to-wall carpet, with linoleum in the service areas, became almost standard. Until recently, Australia and New Zealand tended to follow the English example, but both countries have freed up their approach and now design their buildings according to their needs and climate. These days, floors in Australia and New Zealand are as diverse as the climate and the materials available. In northern and tropical Australia, for example, the Balinese style of beautifully sleek and cool hardwood timber floors has become very popular. In the southern temperate zones, local timbers of pines and various hardwoods are polished and embellished with rugs influenced by central and northern Europe. In the cities, the Mediterranean influence of marble and terracotta has made a big hit, just like Mediterranean food and culture.

As the floor is a dominant feature it can set the tone for the home both in looks and function. It is therefore very important to get it right. Try starting with these considerations:

- Style — how do you want your home to look?
- Cost — can you afford it?
- Function —will it work for the way you live?
- Cleaning and maintenance — do you have enough time to keep it looking great?

These days, with an abundance of different materials available from all over the world, you don't have to be stuck with the local product like our ancient ancestors were. And it's no big deal to change your current floor. There are oodles of options for anything you want to create: a concrete floor can be turned into parquet or can be laid with terracotta tiles; old carpet can be pulled up and the timber polished, varnished or painted; you can lay vinyl in quirky patterns. The sky's the limit. What the floor consists of now should not be an impediment to the type of floor you want in the future. And you may be happy with the existing floor — perhaps it simply needs revitalising.

Carpets, rugs and natural fibre floor coverings

carpets

The word carpets generally refers to those called 'fitted' or 'wall-to-wall'. Rugs and natural fibre coverings will be dealt with separately.

Carpets are available in an ever widening range of styles, textures and materials. Carpet is a perfect insulation material for any room; it holds in the warmth during the winter months and at the same time insulates against the external summertime heat. Carpet also helps to create a peaceful environment because one of its qualities is that it is very good at absorbing sound.

For small children, carpet is the perfect cushion for the inevitable falls that come with learning to crawl or walk. And for the elderly, carpet is a non-slip surface that makes getting around much less hazardous.

Modern quality carpets are manufactured to take the heaviest traffic load that business and public spaces can dish out. So for use in the home there is now a range of very hard wearing carpets that if properly chosen and maintained, will provide many years of enjoyment and use.

Carpet is manufactured on wide looms, which is why it is often sold and quoted by the lineal width or broadloom metre (1 m x 3.67 m). This represents very good value compared to other floor products which are usually sold by the square metre (1 m x 1 m). Broadloom carpet equates to about three times that of a square metre. So when you're getting a quote for a new carpet, make sure it's in broadloom metres.

Choosing a carpet

Deciding on the right carpet for your home may initially appear daunting with the huge choice that is available but it is really only a matter of what type of wear the carpet is likely to have and selecting the colour and style that you like and you can make a decorating investment you'll enjoy for years.

When you begin looking for a carpet, look first for the Australian Carpet Classification Scheme (ACCS) label on the back of the sample. Carpets included in this scheme have passed internationally recognised wear and performance tests and have been examined by an independent panel of experts.

The ACCS covers carpets made from all the major fibres including wool, nylon and polypropylene. In Australia, two other carpet grading schemes operate for carpet made of wool fibre. The Woolmark and Fernmark carpet grading schemes are administered by The Woolmark Company and Wools of New Zealand respectively.

Carpet contributes to the design of the home in the same way the walls and ceiling do — it is a large flat plane of colour and texture that can be an important fashion statement or a background for your furnishings. Carpet is indeed the fifth wall of a room, connecting all the design elements.

Carpets can be selected to be used in two ways:

- the 'feature' approach — incorporating carpet colour as a major decoration feature; or
- the 'background' approach — choosing a carpet colour that will blend with or complement your other decor choices.

When purchasing and laying new carpet, ensure you are provided with a quality underlay. A poor underlay that gives up the ghost before your quality carpet does can make the carpet look old before its time.

While colour is a very personal area of choice it is worth noting that in general, rich colours warm up and close in a room, while cool light colours give a feeling of freshness and space. More subdued colours or earth tones will add a quiet mood to a room.

Remember, it is important to look at large carpet samples in your home, both in daylight and in the evening. As with paints and other furnishings, carpet colours can look quite different under different lighting conditions. Bright natural light and sunlight will make even quite dark colours look pale and washed out while at night these colours will be much darker. Rooms that receive little natural light will benefit from light colours which will lighten the room.

Consider the other elements in the room if you are thinking of choosing a pattern. Elegant patterns with classic motifs will complement dark, polished wood furniture and antiques, while strong colours and geometric patterns make an ideal companion to contemporary furnishings.

Remember that large areas of pattern can make a room seem smaller than it is, while a single light coloured carpet will stretch the dimensions of the room, particularly if the colour complements the wall colours.

Carpet surface and textures

Once you start looking at carpets you will discover the range and variety of textures that are available. There are the thick, heavy carpet yarns used in natural tones in the loop-style Berber carpets. Or the carpets that look like sisal but are actually wool. Then there are cut pile carpets that look like velvet and have a very even and highly finished surface because of the dense tufts and the way the fibre tips have been sheared. There are combinations of cut pile and loops as well as special yarns and finishing processes that are used to achieve a whole range of effects.

There are basically three types of carpet surfaces:

- cut pile;
- loop pile;
- combinations of cut and loop tufts.

- Frieze/hard twist — this is a cut pile carpet made up of highly twisted tufts that curl slightly at the pile surface. The yarn is tightly twisted then heat set, which gives the carpet an interesting textured surface.
- Plush and velvets — a cut pile carpet where the end of each tuft flairs slightly to produce a velvet or plush smooth surface. There are a range of different styles that vary the height of the pile and the amount of flair in the end of each tuft.
- Cut and loop — the carpet is a mixture of loops and tufts. The bunches of higher cut tufts and lower loops form a textured pattern. The cut and loops can come in patterns that imitate the square pattern of tiles or in lines and patterns or can be random.
- Loop/Berber — normally made of thicker yarns in chunky loop tufts — most often these are Berbers, usually in earth tones with a flecked or mottled appearance.

- Sisal — a loop pile carpet that is similar in appearance to sisal or coir matting. The loop lines can be the same height or a pattern of high and low rows.
- Loop — a simple loop pile with tufts of equal height normally in a 'tight' construction using a fairly fine yarn.

Choice of fibre

Carpet is generally made using the following three fibres:

- nylon (polyamide)
- wool
- polypropylene (polyolefin).

Some carpets are made of blends of these fibres; for example 80 per cent wool, 20 per cent nylon is a common blend.

Despite the competing claims of carpet manufacturers no one fibre can claim to be the best for carpet manufacture. And there is no simple answer to the question 'which fibre is best'. There are a range of factors to be taken into consideration when choosing a carpet and the type of fibre is just one of them.

Generally speaking, carpet manufacturers use a particular pile fibre to achieve maximum performance while taking into consideration the cost for the consumer. Manufacturers can produce a carpet for practically any end-use traffic application and budget.

Carpet grading schemes have been designed to take account of these variables and to take the guesswork out of the selection process. The grading scheme can be used to find the right carpet for what you want and then it's a matter of your choice of colour and texture.

Installation and laying

Once you have selected your carpet it is important that the carpet is installed professionally. If it is not professionally laid the manufacturers' warranty might be invalid and, more importantly, if it is not properly installed it may wear quickly and will not look as good as it could.

To work out how much carpet you need so that you can estimate the cost, firstly measure each area. Remember carpet is generally sold in widths of 3.66 metres so, for example, if your room is 4 metres in length and 3 metres wide, you will need 4 metres of carpet and then have it cut down to size. Since each room will not be 3.66 metres wide, you may have to waste carpet or purchase extra pieces to fill in the sides.

The best idea is to make up a floor plan with the measurements of each room and take this to your retailer for a quotation. The retailer or carpet layer will work out exactly how much carpet and how many joins will be needed. The placement of cross-joins and seams is very important because they can detract from the look and performance of your new carpet. Your quotation should include the carpet and underlay, removal of old carpet if that is necessary, moving the furniture if that is necessary and installation of the new carpet.

Carpet underlay is just as important in some ways as the carpet. Underlay improves the cushioning effect of carpet and absorbs some of the compaction on the pile as it is walked on. Underlay also evens out a slightly uneven floor and helps to insulate your home and absorb sound.

The three main types of underlay used today are felt, foam and rubber; your choice will most likely be made on availability, cost and the amount of wear expected.

Don't be tempted to reuse your existing underlay if you are replacing old carpet; the underlay will have the same wear patterns that are apparent in your carpet.

Runners and stair carpets

Stairs are very heavy traffic areas so buy the best quality you can afford. It will be worth it in the long run because of the extra expense to lay carpet on stairs, so you do not want to replace stair carpets more often than is absolutely necessary.

Runner carpets are narrow, central strips usually laid along hallways and galleries, leaving an area of bare floor along either side. If the bare floor area is timber, it can be sanded and finished with polyurethane, paint or varnish and offer a marvellously striking effect. Runners over (or inlaid on) parquet look can look fabulous, and coir or sisal runners can look great laid over painted concrete.

Runners are normally laid so there is about 150–200 millimetres between the edge and the wall and about 300–600 millimetres at either end. If it is inset into a floor, such as parquetry, allow about 7–8 millimetres for the smooth edge — the underlay sits between the strips of smooth edge and the runner is laid on top. Allow about 5–8 millimetres for the thickness of the runner depending on the pile depth. To secure a runner (and rug as well), fix a self-adhesive open weave mat to the underside of the rug to prevent any movement.

Staircases can either be laid with fitted carpet or a runner where the wood on either side can again be sanded and finished with polyurethane, paint or varnish. Normally, stair carpet can be purchased in the ready-made stair widths. Like carpet in rooms stair carpets require underlay, often a non-continuous underlay that overhangs each step and gives the carpet the appearance of tapering back into the stair at the base.

Your local carpet supplier will be able to accurately measure and lay the carpet for you, but if you prefer to lay it yourself, measure along the longest length of any steps and make sure you measure the height of each step as well. Laying a stair runner is easier than a fitted stair carpet, but please take special care if you are laying it yourself. Stair carpets that are not properly and professionally laid can work loose and become quite dangerous.

Vacuuming tips

- Once a new carpet has been laid, it will need to be vacuumed frequently in the first week to collect all the surface lint and loose fluff. There are always some excess loose fibres that have been caught in the carpet during the manufacturing process.
- Most vacuum cleaners come in one of two types — barrel cleaners and upright cleaners. Upright cleaners usually incorporate a pile agitator such as a beater bar or revolving bristle strip that lifts the pile and helps with the removal of dirt and grit. However, be careful with the agitator as over-use can damage the pile surface. Barrel cleaners rely on suction for the removal of dust and lint. Some barrel cleaners have power head attachments to agitate the pile in the same way that upright cleaners do.
- Ensure the vacuum cleaner dust bags are emptied often and that the brushes are cleaned and replaced when worn out, otherwise the vacuum cleaner will not be doing its job properly. Worn brushes will not lift the pile of the carpet and the suction of the vacuum is affected by how much dust is in the dust bag.
- Most vacuum cleaners now come with special filters to remove even very fine dust — these multi filter and micro filter systems ensure that fine particles are removed, which is great for the dust sensitive.
- Vacuum at least weekly to remove soil and grit, which can be abrasive and damage the carpet fibres. In heavy traffic areas vacuum even more often and take extra care. Always vacuum first against the natural direction of the carpet pile — this helps to lift the pile and loosen dirt and grit. Then vacuum in the direction of the pile so that the carpet settles back into a uniform finish.

- **Spot cleaning**
  Always act quickly to mop up spills before they can be absorbed by the carpet fibres and pile.

- **Powder cleaners**
  Powder cleaners are generally used to freshen up carpet but they are not as effective as having carpets cleaned using shampoo or steam. They are applied to the carpet after it has been well vacuumed. The powder is then worked into the carpet with a brush or massaged in with your hand and vacuumed up.

- **Foam shampoos**
  These are ideal for cleaning small areas. The foam is sprayed lightly on the carpet and worked in with a damp cloth, sponge or brush. The carpet is vacuumed once the carpet is dry.

- **Shampoo cleaning**
  Shampoo cleaning refreshes and deodorises the carpet, and lifts the pile. You can employ a professional carpet cleaner or hire a shampoo machine at a department or hardware store. The machines release the shampoo from a tank into a brush. With the action of the brush, the liquid is worked into the carpet pile. The residues are then extracted. For a really good job or for a carpet that is in need of a really good clean the professional cleaners have better equipment and more experience. If you are doing the shampooing yourself, take care only to use recognised and suitable commercial shampoos and cleaners; be careful not to over-wet the carpet; and before you start, do a small test section in an out-of-the-way corner to make sure the cleaning will not harm the carpet and that it has the desired effect. Each commercial product should have directions for use and warnings for the types of carpets for which it may be unsuitable. It's wise to follow these directions

or disasters can happen. Generally speaking, shampooing is a four-step process:

1 Vacuum the carpet.
2 Using a carpet shampooer, apply the shampoo as directed.
3 Make sure the carpet doesn't get too wet.
4 An oft-forgotten trick is to start at the furthest point from the door, working back towards the doorway so you can escape without walking across your newly shampooed carpet.

- **Hot water injection and extraction (steam cleaning)** This is generally recognised as the best way to revitalise and remove deep seated soil and dirt from your carpet. Special injection cleaning and extraction machines are used by skilled professionals for this process. If it is not properly done the carpet can become over-wet, which can permanently damage the carpet and backing materials. Steam cleaning should be carried out every eighteen months, depending on how much traffic the carpet has.

Many of us ripped our carpets up in favour of floorboards in the 1980s and 1990s and some are now going back to carpet. There is an extraordinary range to choose from nowadays; it is warmer if you live in a cool part of Australia and it doesn't skid and ride up underfoot like rugs.

Dealing with carpet disasters

The following table lists some common types of stains and the recommended steps to remove them. In the case of spills, remove the excess spillage immediately by first scraping any solids and blotting liquids with an absorbent material. Use a spoon or blunt knife to remove the bulk of semi-solids or greasy substances and follow this by blotting.

Always begin at the outer edge and work towards the centre of the stained area using a blotting or dabbing motion. After most of the spill has been absorbed, place a fresh pile of paper towels over the area and place a flat weight on them. Never rub a stain.

Use each cleaning method in the sequence listed and follow the 'Do it yourself' actions described above.

SOURCE OF STAIN	NYLON FIBRE CARPET	WOOL FIBRE CARPET	POLYPROPYLENE CARPET
Beverages (tea, coffee, soft drinks)	13, 14, 13, 1	1, 2	
Blood	13, 15, 13, 3	3, 2	5, 1
Chewing gum	16, 6 (3–5 minutes) Repeat if necessary	4	16, 6, 5, 1
Chocolate	13, 15, 13, 1	1, 5	6, 5, 1
Crayon/colour marker	6, 3, 17, 3 Repeat if necessary	6, 2	6, 5, 1
Fruit juice	13, 14, 13, 1	1, 2	5, 1
Furniture polish	6, 13, 1	6, 5, 7	6, 5, 1
Ink (ballpoint pen)	6, 13, 1	18, 2	6, 18, 1
Lipstick	6, 13, 1	6, 2, 1	18, 5, 1, 6
Nail polish	8	8, 6	8
Oil and grease	6, 13, 1	6, 5	6, 5, 1
Paint (oil)	6, 13, 1	9 or 10, 6, 5, 7	9, 6, 5, 1
Shoe polish	6, 13, 1	6, 5	5, 1, 6
Urine (damp)	1, 15, 13, 1	5	5, 1
Urine (dry)	13, 14, 15, 13, 1	7	5, 1
Vomit	19, 13, 15, 13, 1	7	5, 1, 6
Wax (candle)	12 or 16, 6 (3–5 minutes)	11, 6	
Wine (white)	13, 14, 13, 1	1, 2	20, 5, 1
Wine (red)	20, 1, 21	1, 2	20, 5, 1

Cleaning method

1. Clean warm water.
2. Fabric detergent = solution of 1 teaspoon (5 ml) of approved wool detergent with 1 teaspoon of white vinegar and 1 litre of warm water.
3. Clean cold water.
4. Chewing gum remover (freezing agent).
5. Carpet shampoo solution.
6. Dry cleaning fluid. Caution: ensure that no flame or lighted cigarette is near, and use in a well ventilated area.
7. Consult specialist.
8. Nail polish remover — it should not include lanolin or be of a greasy nature.
9. Turpentine.
10. White spirit.
11. Absorbent paper and hot iron.
12. Brown paper and warm iron.
13. Detergent = 1 teaspoon clear dishwashing detergent with 1 cup warm water.
14. Undiluted white vinegar.
15. Ammonia — undiluted household ammonia, foaming type containing detergent.
16. Freeze with ice cube, shatter with blunt object and vacuum clean.
17. Solution = water and non-bleach mild detergent.
18. Methylated spirits. Caution: ensure that no flame or lighted cigarette is near, and use in a well ventilated area.
19. Baking soda, scrape and vacuum.
20. Absorbent powder (salt). Sprinkle on spillage, leave overnight and vacuum next day.
21. Dye stripper. Dilute 50 to 1 with cold water. Caution: Do not use on dark or patterned carpet.

Source: The Carpet Institute of Australia Ltd

Rugs

Chinese ➢ contemporary ➢ dhurries ➢ flokati ➢ kelims ➢ Persian ➢ Portuguese needlepoint ➢ rag ➢ Tibetan ➢ Turkish

Rugs are a fabulous alternative to fitted carpet and look great strewn across a polished timber floor. They can bring a certain brightness and 'attitude' to decorating a room — they're a real statement.

There are so many different types of rugs that you can find one to suit any budget. Some dhurry-styled cotton rugs, which come from India, are extremely cheap. Cheap rag rugs are available too. Alternatively, you could commission a master craftsman to weave a rug to your own specifications.

As with everything else, quality is an issue so it's good to be aware of what constitutes a quality hand-made rug. First, take a look at the pattern: it should be even, bright and well defined. If not you're probably looking at a printed reproduction. Second, check the quality of the wool: there may be a certification attached that guarantees its quality. Third, look at the back of the rug and check the density of the knots — the more knots per square centimetre the better.

Before committing to a rug, try it out in your room — if it doesn't quite work change things around. When you lay a rug it's important to have the right underlay; it's no good having a rug that slips all over the place, which can be dangerous. Ask your retailer for advice on the best options. And another tip: reposition the rug from time to time so it wears evenly. Bright, vividly coloured rugs can certainly make the grand statement in a room. Give them a try; you just might be surprised how well it works when you never thought it would.

Rug types

- **Chinese:** normally quite expensive, these sumptuous rugs made of silk and wool are available in a marvellous range of colours from blues and black to apricots and pinks. They often include Chinese motifs such as butterflies, dragons and lotus blossom.

- **Contemporary:** contemporary rugs come in as many designs, types and colours as there are people to create them. Some are manufactured using the latest technologies and machinery, while others are handwoven by artists and craftspeople. A handcrafted rug can be an item of great beauty in your home.
- **Dhurry:** dhurries are flat, woven rugs from India. They usually come in pastel colours — blues, pinks, greens and whites — and feature various geometric designs with borders. They are mostly made of cotton, although the more expensive ones have additions of silk and wool.
- **Flokati:** this is the creamy white shaggy-dog pile rug that was so often placed in front of open fires in the 1980s, but of course it can be used anywhere and makes a great bedroom rug. Colours are usually in creams but greys are also available.

Drape antique rugs like kelims over chairs or couches, or reuse worn out rugs to make floor cushions — they will add colour to an otherwise ordinary room.

- **Kelim:** kelims are non-pile, tapestry-woven rugs made in Russia, Yugoslavia, Afghanistan and Turkey. Made usually from wool, the Afghan version is thicker and features muted colours and simple designs, whereas the Turkish styles are mainly thinner with somewhat brighter designs that sometimes feature embroidery as well. Kelims can be hugely expensive — many are collector's items.
- **Persian:** rich reds, blues, blacks, creams and their distinctive geometrical designs, we've all come across a Persian rug at one time or another. Persian rugs can be either hand-made in wools and silks or manufactured and range from expensive to really expensive. Beware of those cheap imitations that sell in markets all around the world — they are not authentic.
- **Portuguese needlepoint:** these are coarser, hand-woven rugs that more often than not feature a floral design. Bright, refined and hard wearing, Portuguese needlepoints can bring a wonderful, luxurious charm to a room, especially when set off against natural and rustic colours.
- **Rag rugs:** rag rugs have often been associated with the pioneering families of the United States — the craft probably travelling from Europe with the early settlers — however, they occur in many societies throughout the world. Rags rugs, as the name suggests, normally use old cast-offs as their raw materials — old clothes, blankets and other scraps of textiles — to make many different weaves and colour combinations.
- **Tibetan:** Tibet's isolation means we probably don't see as many rugs as we could from this traditional rug-making country. What we do see is often made by Tibetan emigres living in other parts of the world. The

subdued patterns, colours and designs offer an alternative to the richer Persian and kelim styles.

- **Turkish:** Turkish rugs, with their rich deep blues and reds, are often made as prayer rugs but tend also to comprise four main styles. The first is the hand-made pure silk carpet that is named after the region in which it is made. Often featuring a floral pattern, they sometimes have a gold thread woven though them making them truly 'fit for a king'. The second is cotton and wool, made by knotting the wool on a cotton base. The third is the wool — often used as prayer rugs — where vegetable dyes create subtle delicate colours. And fourth, there are kelims as discussed above. Kelims were an essential part of a young woman's dowry and were used on floors, as curtains, room dividers, cradle and lounge covers and prayer rugs.

Tips on cleaning rugs

- Antique and valuable rugs: don't shampoo or wash antique or valuable rugs at home — call in an expert. For everyday cleaning, use a carpet sweeper or give it a gentle 'beating'. Drape the rug over the clothesline and beat it gently with the flat side of a straw broom or use an old tennis racquet — practise your forehand! Do not use a vacuum cleaner.
- Furs and skins: if you must have animal furs and skins on your floor instead of them running around in the wild, then don't shampoo them or immerse them in water. Take a mild detergent dissolved in water and sponge the hide a small section at a time, leaving each section to dry before starting the next.
- Long-haired rugs: wash a small corner only in tepid water using a very mild detergent and thoroughly rinse with a little fabric softener. Dry outside in the shade. When dry, gently tease the fibres. If a small section works, do the whole carpet. If not, reconsider trying to do it yourself.

Carpet tiles

Carpet tiles are normally used in offices and other commercial buildings these days where they are often simply stuck to the concrete floor. However, they can also be used at home laid over underfelt. They are available in wool and nylon, cut pile and tufted loop, and are of various 'weights'. Carpet tiles have two main advantages: they can be rotated to even out wear and tear; and they can be laid in various patterns including border patterns. The new styles are worth considering.

Natural fibres — sisal and coir

These natural fibre 'carpets' and mats, especially when teamed with the right textures in walls and furnishings, can make a fabulously striking floor covering. Gone are the days when the ubiquitous seagrass matting, fraying and tatty, covered the floors of university students in our inner suburbs. The modern sisals and coirs offer a stunning array of quality floor coverings with beautifully restrained 'natural' colours and textures.

Sisal is made from the fibre as rope — from the leaf fibres of the agave plant — whereas coir is made from the fibres of the outer husk of the outer shell. Both are hard wearing and resilient and very reasonable in price. The better quality sisals and coirs are backed with a rubber or latex underlay, which has a good cushioning effect and makes them much easier to clean. If there is one criticism of coir and sisal it is that their toughness can be hard underfoot or can graze the skin off knees. But their beautifully natural, warm, honeyed colours make for a striking appearance — especially when teamed with natural, sometimes rustic furniture and natural-looking ceilings and walls.

Modern natural floor coverings are not difficult to clean and many manufacturers and stockists recommend an upright vacuum cleaner with a moving brush or power head. Clean along the direction of the top fibres for the best results. The woven texture of the natural carpet is very dense so it is unlikely dust and dirt will be deep in the pile as it can be with a conventional carpet.

Timber floors

Our current house was rented for many years before we moved in and on the floor was a deeply repulsive, sickly green carpet that had been worn down to the consistency of felt. It had to go, but the floorboards underneath weren't much better — the floor sander told me he had to use a couple of kilos of 'filler' to pack the gaps. Happily, he did a great job, and if he hadn't told me about the gaps I wouldn't have noticed them.

He left the floor looking splendid, all shiny and new. Eighteen months and two young boys, two big dogs and two cats later, it's looking a bit the worse for wear. Lots of scratches and there's nothing like a timber floor (except perhaps marble!) to show how long it is since you swept.

If you opt for floorboards and you want to tackle the sanding yourself, my advice is — practise somewhere else first! It's not as easy as it looks and can be dangerous. We had one room in another house that an inexperienced friend tried to do that ended up with more peaks and troughs than a big dipper.

Hardwood and softwood floorboards

Timber flooring can be constructed of hardwood or softwood or parquet. It then needs to be sanded. Once that's done, you can choose what you want to do.

It is important to understand that timber floors are a completely natural material. And that natural timber is hygroscopic — it continually takes up and releases moisture in balance with its surroundings. If you live in a moist environment the timber will retain a lot of moisture. If you live in a dry environment it will retain little moisture. This process results in the timber in your floor undergoing a natural shrinkage and expansion. To reduce the amount of shrinkage and expansion, timber flooring is usually seasoned or kiln dried to an average

moisture content of between 10 per cent and 15 per cent. This level of moisture is suitable for the majority of installations. However, in some locations the timber may need to be acclimatised, that is, delivered some time before installation so that the timber adjusts its moisture content prior to being installed.

Timber for floorboards is usually sawn, seasoned and machined into boards called 'tongue and groove'; this allows the boards to slot together, forming a sealed floor.

Choosing the right timber floor for your home will end up being a personal choice of what will suit your home style and the colour and finish you like, but you will find there is a huge selection from which to choose. Some tips to remember are that the general colour of the wood is determined by the timber species. However, even with one species there will be variations. Some species remain mostly true to type while others vary greatly. Because it is a natural product your floor will be completely unique. Depending on the species chosen, various combinations of timber boards could be available. You may like the idea of featuring all the natural variations such as knots, gum veins (generally dark lines) and insect markings; or you may choose boards that have variations in their colour so your floor will clearly show the boards; or you may wish the floor to be consistently the same colour and effect. Discuss this with your flooring specialist so that you are not disappointed with the result.

The actual colour of a floor will only become evident after it has been sanded and coated with your chosen finish. But flooring specialists have samples that will show you how the various finishes will affect the colour of the floor.

Remember that a darker floor will make the room appear darker, and may therefore require more available daylight and/or artificial light. Lighter coloured floors tend to show dirt and marks less than darker floors.

Some people swear that second-hand timber flooring is much cheaper than new, but before you rush out to a demolition yard do your sums. Can you get the amount you need, and by the time you've spent hours of your time driving to the demo yard selecting, loading, unloading, cleaning and de-nailing the flooring, would it be easier and cheaper to just order them new? Your time is worth money and should always be factored into the 'bargain' price of second-hand building materials.

Timber floors can last a lifetime if you follow a few basic rules: wipe up spills as soon as they happen; sweep or wipe up sand or grit immediately; use mats to stop dirt and grit being brought into the house.

Older houses may have existing timber floors that have been oiled, varnished, waxed or finished with shellac, and you may want to merely refurbish the existing finish. Restoring a floor in that way is a great option. The most frequently used and popular finish these days is polyurethane, often known by one of its many brand names. However, there are a fantastic number of old and new options available.

You should always seek local professional advice before making your final choice.

Discuss all the points on the timber flooring checklist with your chosen flooring specialists; they will also be able to advise on the need for on-site acclimatisation. Choose your timber carefully, considering the following:

Checklist for new timber floors

- colour/timber species
- any special timber features
- end result required
- top or secret nails
- hardness/foot traffic
- board width and laying direction

Timber finish selection

- tung oil, subdued/semi-gloss
- polyurethane, hard, smooth, glossy
- liming/stains
- glossy surface reflections
- style requirements for period housing

Home design considerations

- vents or drains in floors
- air-conditioning
- direct sunlight
- dry or humid climate

Parquet has a wonderful elegance and luxurious feel about it and looks great in hallways, lounge rooms and dining rooms. It can consist of small blocks or 'fingers' of a single timber or a number of hardwoods and softwoods arranged together to make various patterns. Squares and herringbone patterns are the most popular designs, and with its mix of grains and colours it can look spectacular.

There are a number of different types of parquet generally available — mosaic, block, end grain block and floor tile types made by slicing veneer block to a designed thickness and machining tongues and grooves to give an interlocking tile-like module.

Mosaic parquet is made from thin fingers of wood typically about 100–150 mm long, 20 mm wide and 9 mm thick. The fingers are joined to make a conveniently sized module (or panel) in varying patterns and timbers.

Block parquet is made from longer, wider and thicker pieces of wood than the mosaic 'fingers', and similarly assembled into modules and panels.

End grain parquet provides very different patterns using the end of the wood rather than across the grain. It is often used for floor areas where extremely hard wear is expected.

Parquet can be installed on most surfaces as long as they are dry and stable. Various underlays are used depending on the base and its stability. The parquet is then glued into position using parquet-specific adhesives, allowed to dry, sanded, then finished as for other timber floors.

Chipboard

Another timber flooring choice is particleboard or chipboard. Chipboard has the great advantage of being cheap to buy and quick and easy to install. Although some people feel the chipboard appearance can look a little makeshift, especially with a clear finish, it has excellent durability and is great for the kids' rooms and rumpus rooms. With its darkish, golden look, which doesn't show up dust and lint, polyurethane makes the best clear finish while painting and stencilling can look even better.

Bamboo

Strictly speaking bamboo is not a timber; it's a fast growing grass. In fact it's the fastest growing plant on earth and grows so fast you can almost 'see' it growing! And that's what makes it so interesting as a flooring material — after it's harvested it grows again quickly, and that, in environmental terms, is known as a 'renewable resource'. Whereas a hardwood tree takes 40 to 60 years to grow and is lost in the harvesting, bamboo takes only four to six years to grow and retains its root system for rapid regeneration. It is harvested for manufacturing after between four to five years.

The cane used for flooring is the big, thick bamboo, not the thin cane you see used for furniture. Bamboo is grown in abundance in the provinces of southern China and in other parts of Asia. The manufacturing process includes treatment for the removal of sugar, mildew and insects.

Bamboo is available in a number of colours ranging from light to dark, prefinished with polyurethane or unfinished. It can be installed like tongue and groove timber boards or as a floating floor and it's also available in parquet modules.

Choosing the best finish for timber board floors

Liming and stains ➢ paint ➢ polyurethane ➢ shellac ➢ tung oil ➢ varnish ➢ wax

Timber finishes fall into two basic types: penetrating finishes and surface finishes. Determining the best finish for your timber floor depends on its current condition, your personal preference, whether it is a light or heavy traffic area and the time you want to spend for care and maintenance.

Checklist for existing timber floors

- current condition of floor/tongue and groove?
- timber species and features
- house style
- floor use, durability required (foot traffic)
- home design considerations — under-floor ventilation and drainage, air-conditioning, skylights/direct sunlight through large windows
- finish selection — tung oil (subdued, semi-gloss), polyurethane (hard, smooth, glossy), liming/stains, surface reflections, refurbishing requirements
- care and maintenance.

Liming and stains

Timber board floors are great because there are so many stunning effects you can achieve. 'Liming' or whitening a timber board floor looks great, when either done in the traditional diamond pattern using two matching or contrasting colours or simply using one colour throughout. Liming solutions come in many milky pastels easily tinted to your desired colour. As well, oil-based 'white washes' can be used for liming directly onto a sanded, unsealed timber floor to give a great smoky effect to the grain. Usually, coats of polyurethane or another finish are then applied over the top for extra durability. Liming can be done yourself, but make sure you get professional advice before you start.

You can use acrylic artist's paints too, to add slight 'tints' to your timber floor. This can create the same effect as 'liming' a floor and you can mix exactly the colour you want. You will need to have sanded floorboards, then mix your paints together with water to make the colour you want. Brush the wash along the grain and rub the colour back using a clean cloth. Leave the wash to completely dry, then finish with an acrylic varnish. It is a good idea to do a test first so that you will know just how much colour will create the effect you want. If you are unhappy with the colour you can sand it back before applying the varnish.

If you're planning to sand your timber floor but you're just not happy with its natural colour, try staining it with a wood stain. Stains can be used either to change the floor colour completely or to modify and enhance the present colour — and it's a good solution if you want to match your floor to other woodwork and your furniture for instance. You can also do great 'design tricks' like staining alternate floorboards different colours. Now, there's a look. Check out your specialty paint store or flooring adviser; there is a great range of stains available in just about any natural timber colour. Normally, the floor needs to be sanded first and the surface finished with varnish, wax or polyurethane.

Oils

Oils can give a floor a beautiful matt finish and have the advantage of being easy to apply and easy to repair if it becomes scuffed by the kids' basketball boots or dad's golf shoes. Tung oil, a derivative of the Chinese nut tree, is the most widely used, but Scandinavian oil and linseed oils are also sometimes used. Some experts consider oils too thin for open grain timbers and they can require several coats to buff up to a good, sound surface. As well, they may need to be re-applied regularly, say twice a year, for the floor to maintain its tip top appearance. Not the best of finish for heavy traffic areas, oils can be hardened by a coat of wax or special hardening polishes. However, the waxing has the disadvantage of having to be removed before re-oiling.

One of the great things about oils is that they have an inviting scent or can be scented using dried herbs to give a beautiful, fresh lift to the house every time you mop the floor. Linseed oil has its own distinctively pleasant smell — familiar to all those dads who played cricket in their youth — although some people find that it remains too 'oily' and doesn't 'dry'.

Infuse your flooring oil or wax with a herb to make a beautiful and natural deodorant. Some herbs, such as basil, are said to deter flies and other insects. What could be better than a floor cleaner, deodorant and insect repellent in one!

Paint

Painting is a very attractive solution as a floor finish. The colours, of course, are unlimited, and you can also use patterns and stencils to create fabulous centrepieces and borders. There are floor paints available for every surface; and for chipboard and concrete floors, painting can be a great solution. Make sure you get advice on the right type of paint for your particular surface.

A colour that doesn't show up dust and dirt too much is always a good idea, and this can be embellished by a stencilled pattern along the edges — ideal for the kids' rooms.

Stencilling

Stencils and centrepieces are usually do-it-yourself jobs and can be applied direct to sanded floorboards or hardboard, or to varnished or painted floors. Make sure you finish with three coats of polyurethane or varnish or your work will soon vanish like a sidewalk drawing.

For stencilling, take a piece of paper or light card and draw up your design using a pencil and ruler. Put it in place on the floor to check if you like it, whether it's the right size and how many times you will need to apply it for the length of floor. Once you are satisfied, cut out the stencil from either light card or a firm piece of plastic the same weight as light cardboard (the advantage is that plastic is washable). Place the stencil in position. Taping the edges in place is a good idea. Take a suitably sized brush (smaller is better than bigger), dip it in your chosen colour, pat the brush on the edge of the can to remove all excess paint and brush swiftly and lightly across the stencil, remembering to hold it perfectly still. Carefully remove the stencil and paint the next one — a string or light pencil line can give you a reference point to make sure your pattern is straight.

Another stencilling approach is to use a stipple effect with a dry brush. For this use a thick dry brush and a small quantity of paint on the brush. Dab the end of the brush over the stencil. You can use different colours with this technique so long as the colours do not come in contact with one another.

Creating a centrepiece is a little more adventurous, but it can be quite easily done and offers a real sense of achievement for the whole family once completed. Centrepieces can be big, huge or small and are mostly geometrical in design — but don't let that stop you if the free-form approach is more your style. A centrepiece is best designed directly onto the floor, but before you start do a rough sketch of what you want to do. Use a pencil and some drawing equipment to help you with straight and curved lines. When you're happy with your design, grab your paints and start 'colouring' it in. When painting adjoining areas it's often best to wait until the first area is dry.

Centrepieces and stencils can be very rewarding and can become a cherished piece of family art in the home.

Polyurethane

Clear, plastic-based polyurethane, in all its various brand names, is the most popular finish for timber floors simply because it's the toughest and easiest to maintain. Quick and economical to apply, it is ideal for heavy traffic areas but, be warned, even this tough finish is not impervious to the scratching and gouging of sandy little feet, teenagers' clumsiness and parents' accidents.

When polyurethane surfaces get damaged they cannot be repaired other than by removing that section of the finish and starting again — that is, by resanding the floor and refinishing. It can only be applied to sanded floors (it won't work with chemically stripped floors) and is perhaps a little plastic looking for an older home. Nevertheless, when it comes to that modern, bright, airy look polyurethane, with its fabulously easy-to-maintain finish, really does have the goods.

Polyurethane has one other important characteristic: when applied it soaks down between the gaps in the boards, completely sealing the floor.

Don't overdo the colour when stencilling some of the most effective designs are quite minimal in their use of colour.

Problems

Timber is a natural material whose moisture content is influenced by the ambient moisture content of the air and its surroundings. Where dry joined timbers are used it is important that any sealant permits free movement to allow for any expansion, contraction or movement in the timber.

When there is free movement in the joints the changes in the timber are hardly noticeable. But if a sealant gets between the dry joints and bonds the boards together this can result in some of the boards splitting under the pressure of the movement or groups of boards that are joined together moving away from an adjoining set of boards creating gaps in the floor.

Polyurethane sealants can sometimes bond or glue boards together so prior to applying a sealant, seek advice first.

Shellac

Shellac will be known to many people as French polish — although the flooring version is specific to this use and applied differently. Shellac is one of the most natural wood finishes and is made from a tiny South-East Asian scale insect known as *Laccifer lacca*. The insect produces a resinous secretion found on the branches of specific trees called 'lac' which means 'hundred thousand', as it takes 40,000 to 200,000 insects to produce 1 kilogram of shellac. It can be applied to chemically stripped and sanded floors and may be applied over previous coats without any problems. Shellac has that special finish, or patina, that makes it very suitable for older homes. It has a toughness, too, that makes it fine to use in moderate traffic areas anywhere in the house, except wet service areas such as the kitchen and bathroom. Give shellac a coat of wax and it will harden even more; and instead of re-shellacking as the finish becomes scuffed, you simply buff or re-wax.

Sanding a floor

Sanding a timber floor is a big job because first you have to remove all the furniture from the room, including the curtains ... and yes, the piano has to go too. And besides, if your house is like mine, you won't have anywhere to put it all. By far the best alternative is to have a professional floor sander come and do it for you, but if you're the handy type or you want to save money, here is a step by step guide:

1. Get some local and professional advice.
2. Remove all the furniture and fittings (it is going to get very dusty).
3. Sweep or vacuum the floor.
4. With a nail punch, punch in all the floorboard nails a sufficient distance so the sander won't hit them. Sanding belts get ripped to bits on nails! Remove all excess nails and tacks such as carpet tacks.
5. Hire a floor sander and an edging sander.
6. Sand with a coarse grade belt working with the grain and being careful not to damage the skirting boards. Use a smaller sander for that.
7. Sand the edges with a matching coarse grade paper.
8. Fill the nail holes with filler.
9. Repeat the sanding process with medium and fine grades until you are satisfied with the surface.
10. Sweep and vacuum all the dust, then wipe over the floor with a rag to remove any dust that is left. Don't wet the floor — it might stain.
11. Apply your preferred finish.

Parquet floors or mosaic designs pose another problem. Because they are laid in patterns, the grain usually lies in two different directions. The floor, therefore, must be sanded twice: once in the direction of the one grain and then in the direction of the other. The floor must then be sanded with a very fine belt, again in both directions, to remove any scratch marks.

Varnish

After polyurethane, varnish is the toughest timber floor finish and can give you many years of trouble-free wear and tear. It also has a less 'plasticy' look than polyurethane. Once upon a time it left a clear finish and so it first required the application of a stain for any colour modification. These days varnishes can be tinted for any number of special effects and it has the added advantage of being able to be waxed for extra toughness again — making it a very close call between it and polyurethane. Talk to a flooring adviser about all the possibilities with varnish, both oil based and water based.

Wax

Like oiling, waxing a timber floor is a beautifully natural way of creating a stunning finish; and with the wide range of modern products available, you can create any number of effects. There's something about the quality of a waxed floor that gives it a look all of its own — and the wax soaking into the timber, enriching it and keeping it healthy. Before the invention of modern household appliances and high-quality waxes, waxing was seen as time consuming and hard work — people used to have to do it on their knees, and plenty of 'elbow grease' was required! But now, with the right appliances and modern waxes, it can be a simple job. And when the waxed floor becomes scuffed and scratched all you need to do is buff it.

Waxes are now offering many modern flooring effects. For instance, a very smart whitened effect can be achieved by mixing beeswax with titanium (the white oxide pigment used as a colour base for paints) and turpentine — perfect for the informal Mediterranean look. Talk to your local flooring professional or home improvements store for the latest in modern waxing. Like oil, it's a great natural alternative to petroleum-based products.

Tips for timber floors

- For applying oils and maintaining your oiled floor, try using a lamb's wool applicator. It gives excellent results.
- If you're applying polyurethane or varnish to a floor yourself, use a new brush or applicator. Old brushes and applicators drop hairs and lint, making the job that much harder.
- Try not to slide heavy furniture across a varnished or polyurethaned floor; it will soon make scratches and gouge marks in your beautiful finish. Pick furniture up to move it and just to be sure, fit nylon glides and felt tips to the legs of tables and chairs.
- Sweep the floor regularly to remove grit. Scratches are the big enemy of polished timber floors.

Cleaning tips

- For polyurethane use water with a light detergent.
- Never use water to clean waxed, polished or oiled timber finishes.
- Normally, timber finishes are cleaned with a mop dampened with furniture oil, but please check with a professional first for the best cleaner for your floor.

Laminates and floating floors

If you feel that all the preparation and maintenance of a natural timber floor is too much trouble but you still want the timber look, a laminated floating floor may be your answer.

Laminates are normally hard wearing, scratch and burn resistant, repel termites and other insects, are allergy free and are available in easily manageable pack sizes. There is zero maintenance and only minimal cleaning is required. They are usually quick and easy to install, many brands utilising easy 'snap together' sections that require no glue and yet are completely sealed; and the floor can even be taken up and relaid if you move house or change your mind later on.

Floating floors can be laid over virtually any surface, whether it be timber, particleboard or concrete, as long as it's reasonably smooth and level. They are often made of laminated prefinished timber or other stylish finishes, so once the floor is laid it can be used immediately. There is no sanding, waxing or polyurethaning — once it's laid, it's done. There are various products on the market, all using the latest technologies to produce economical easy-to-install floors. Each product is different so it's smart to thoroughly check out all the products available for the one most suited to your needs.

Vinyl and linoleum

The baby boomers would all recognise the name, linoleum, or its more common form, 'lino'. Almost every kitchen in Australia had lino on the floor in the 1950s and 1960s. Lino was constructed of resins, linseed oil, cork and wood and was really the forerunner of the modern 'resilient' class of flooring, now the domain of vinyl and cork.

Vinyl (full name: polyvinyl chloride or PVC) comes in two types: sheet and tile. Sheet vinyl is very quick to install, while tiles offer the opportunity for unlimited pattern and colour combinations. Square or geometric patterns, diamond patterns, small diamonds to offset larger squares, contrasting colours, matching colours — the list is endless. There are also a myriad of imitation patterns, especially available in sheet vinyl — imitation timber, brick, stone, marble, terrazzo, terracotta, to name a few. And vinyl has many fabulous qualities: it's flexible, stain resistant and easy to look after.

Vinyl ➢ cork ➢ ceramic ➢ quarry and terracotta ➢ slate ➢ marble ➢ terrazzo ➢ granite ➢ concrete ➢ brick

Tiles

It doesn't matter whether they are vinyl, ceramic, terracotta or one of the many stones, tiles are a great floor solution. They come into their own in the kitchen, bathroom and laundry, and often work well in lounge rooms, dining rooms and bedrooms too especially in the tropics, where their cool, clean feel underfoot makes them very popular. Marble is also a good option for entrances, lounge rooms and dining rooms for a more formal look.

Tiles offer several functional features:

- They are easy to clean: a quick sweep, a vacuum, a mop with an appropriate cleaner and they're clean again.
- They are hard wearing and durable, making them great for heavy traffic areas.
- Their tough surface makes them resistant to scuffs and scratches.

The other great advantage of tiles is the range of decor opportunities they offer; there is an infinite choice of materials, colours, patterns and designs. You can create virtually anything you want.

Vinyl tiles

You can understand why vinyl tiles are the most popular choice for the family kitchen and laundry when you make a list of all their features. First, you can create all the patterns and designs in the world ranging from extremely simple and natural through bright, colourful and eccentric to stone and crystal effects. You can go 1950s or ultra modern, you can go stylish or outlandish and you can

alter the spatial feeling of the room by the direction in which you lay the tiles. There are lots of different textures, so they feel great underfoot, and they're soft too, so when that glass or precious cup gets accidentally dropped, there's a good chance it won't get broken. Yet they're extremely hard wearing — resistant to water, grease and most domestic products — and they're quiet and act as a buffer against noise.

How many tiles do I need?

So, the old floor covering in the kitchen is looking a bit tired and it's time to replace it, this time with tiles. One of the first things you'll want to know is how much it will cost; and to know that you have to work out how many tiles will be needed to do the job. Here are some tips.

1 Tiles are available from all over the world and some are manufactured in metric sizes while others are in imperial sizes. Therefore, it's worth doing your measurements in both scales.
2 Measure the room and calculate the area in square metres (m^2) and square feet (ft^2). If your floor is an irregular shape, that is, it has a bench jutting out into the room or it has an alcove, you may need to break the room down into sections that allow you to easily calculate the size.
3 It's not a bad idea to make a plan of your room to scale on graph paper. (Pick that up from your local art supplier, stationer or good newsagent.) It can help you with your calculations, your design and to communicate your ideas to retailers and tradespeople.
4 When you select your tiles, or you're simply calling up on the phone to get some ballpark prices, you'll quickly be able to find out how many tiles there are to the square metre (or foot). Multiply this by the number of square metres (feet) in your room to get the total. Add 5 per cent for wastage and errors.

Laying a vinyl tile floor

Laying a vinyl tile floor is probably best left to a professional, but it is possible to do it yourself. Here are some pointers you could consider before taking the big leap and, remember, please seek expert advice. You can't beat it.

1 Preparing the floor so it is completely flat is a crucial stage in laying tiles — the floor must be dead smooth. The normal procedure, unless you are working on a completely smooth and dry cement slab, is to lay an underlay of hardboard such as masonite or fibre cement. It's a bit risky laying tiles directly onto floorboards unless the floor is perfectly even, flat and stable.

2 Thoroughly sweep and vacuum the floor so it is free of dust and grit. If you've got several batches of tiles, take them out of their boxes and mix them up so you don't get colour variances between different lots. Install a string line down the centre of your floor, so it is equidistant from the two longest walls. The tiles will be laid outwards from this line towards the walls.

3 Lay the tiles out on the floor loosely without adhesive, starting from the centre line. This is so you can check how they cover joins in the underlay and how they shape up at the edges. Adjust the centre line if necessary to avoid corresponding joins between the tiles and the underlay. Tile joins should be at least 80 mm from underlay joins if possible. Avoid too narrow a line of tiles at the wall.

4 Now the sticking down job begins. Be careful to follow the directions on your tile product. This will call for cutting some tiles for the walls and edges around benches, etc., for which there are specific techniques. Ask your tile retailer for their recommendations. A handy tip it that the cut edge of the tile should always be laid against the wall or fixture, not the neighbouring tile.

5 Complete the job by walking around the floor to make sure the tiles are firmly in place. Remove any excess glue. You're done.

Cork tiles

Cork is one of those extraordinary natural products. Produced almost exclusively in Portugal, cork is the bark or the outer casing of the trunk of the cork oak (*Quercus suber*). The tree takes a long time to produce — cork is first harvested when the tree is about 25 years old, and subsequently about every nine years. The natural material then goes through a refining and manufacturing process before you see the end product in wine bottles, as noticeboards and on floors.

Like vinyl, modern cork flooring is a 'resilient' floor covering. It is also available in a variety of colours and styles. Cork is a very good insulation material and stays warm in winter and remains cool in summer. It also absorbs sound and resists the indents made by furniture. It can handle a number of different finishes and spills wipe up easily. Cork is now manufactured in such a way that the tiles can appear seamless, which looks very effective.

There are products available now that avoid the need for sanding and revarnishing. After three or four years, you simply mop on a refresh polish and the floor will look like new. Some suppliers say that even after many years you can resurface cork and bring it back to its original shine.

Ceramic tiles

Generally speaking, ceramic tiles are made of a clay base coated with a liquid glaze; this is the standard (or traditional) issue. The tiles are then fired in a kiln at a high temperature, which sets the glaze into a hard non-porous surface. Tiles that have patterns may be fired several times, once for each part of the pattern; and tiles for different purposes, such as floors and walls, go through slightly different processes but the principle is the same. Obviously, floor tiles have to be tougher.

Ceramic tiles are immensely popular. They work in just about any room in the house, but are especially popular in bathrooms, laundries and kitchens. Don't be afraid, however, to consider them for entranceways, lounge rooms, dining rooms and bedrooms. They can really look elegant and charming.

Ceramics give us the opportunity to create great design solutions as well. The all white bathroom with a single tiled frieze around the walls in rich blues or black, and the most simple shower walled only in glass, can look fantastic. Then there's the charm of the tiny glass tiles, the deco style of the 1940s and 1950s. Try doing a bathroom in these with blues and purples playing off each other — the light blue bath, the glass and chrome shower recess, the recessed purple soap dishes and the painted cloud ceiling. It looks amazing. Or a ceramic tiled kitchen featuring a huge mosaic. There are so many solutions that, when you decide to do ceramic tiles, you are really becoming your own artist and interior designer.

Ceramic tiles come in several different types:

- Monocottura: a single-fired ceramic tile that is fully vitrified. Vitrified tiles are made of ground clay combined with stone, such as feldspar and quartz, and fired to a high temperature. This results in tiles of very low porosity that are dense throughout, making them very suitable for heavy traffic areas. Vitrified tiles can be matt or polished, however, the polishing removes some of the outer vitrified surface, reducing the tile's hardness and stain resistance.
- Bicottura: a ceramic tile that is fired twice and is also fully vitrified.
- Standard: tiles of an average measurement and price and a plain colour, that is, about 150 mm x 150 mm for a floor tile and about 200 mm x 200 mm for a wall tile.

- Tessellated: a period tile used for restorations on old buildings, often for highly patterned or mosaic floors.

There's quite a bit to ceramic floor tiling, so keep in mind the various steps and possible pitfalls. Like all home improvements, planning is the key. But an important thing to remember with ceramic tiles, because they are often imported in small lots, is to make sure you have sufficient tiles to do the job. If you're using a combination of different sized tiles, working out the numbers can be a bit fiddly. Draw out a plan or pattern to scale on a large piece of graph paper; it will really help in your calculations. And check out 'How many do I need?' on page 49 — the same basic rules apply.

As with other flooring types preparation is the key, but especially with ceramic tiles, because if there's any movement at all underneath they will soon become dislodged and even break. Tiles have to be laid on a non-rigid surface. If there's any doubt at all put down an underlay such as fibre cement, which is generally considered the best.

If you're planning on tiling a floor in a wet area there is an easy first decision: only use tiles that don't get slippery when they're wet. The trick is that some tiles have a textured surface; they're often the ones that don't slip. Wet the one you like and give it a brake test — see if you can slide a rubber-soled sports shoe over it. If it slides easily it's no good; if it sticks you're probably okay. But ask your tile retailer — they'll be able to help you. Slipping over in the bathroom is a nasty and dangerous business, so please check your tiles out carefully.

If you already have tiles in a wet area that are causing you concern because of their slipperiness, there are companies and tradespeople who can fix the problem for you. It takes specialist equipment and knowledge and it's definitely not a job for the do-it-yourselfer.

The next step in wet areas is to make sure the water doesn't seep away through cracks in the floor, along edges where the floors meet the walls, or those wettest of places, shower recesses. It's a good idea to get a professional to help you plan it and probably tile it as well. This way you can get a guarantee from the company or tradesperson, so if anything does go wrong the work can be repaired at least cost to you.

Tips for tile repairs

- Drummy tiles: the reason tiles sound hollow or 'drummy' is that they have become unstuck. There are a number of reasons why this occurs. One is that the glue has become old and simply stopped working. Another is that the tiles have been laid too close together and expansion and contraction against each other has loosened them. Remove the tile and scrape away all the old glue; replace the tile using a flexible adhesive.
- Mould: mould in grout is a perennial problem for tiles, especially in hot, humid climates. Try using a commercial bathroom cleaner, grout cleaner or bleach. If the problem persists try a commercial grout sealer. Your local tile retailer will be able to advise you.

- Decaying grout: with age and incessant cleaning grout can become old and flaky and start to crack away. With floors, grout is often cement, so scrape out the loose grout, mix up a batch of new grout and fill the gaps. Talk to your tile retailer for some hints; it's pretty easy.

Quarry and terracotta tiles

This group of unglazed clay tiles, generally known as 'quarry' and 'terracotta', are fired from an unrefined clay rich in aluminium (bauxite), giving them their rustic-looking, earthy colours. They're often used for outside paving, but they also look a treat in a country-style kitchen, their warm colours and dull sheen creating a casual, hand crafted charm especially when laid a little 'unevenly'. The Mediterranean look of terracotta has become a favourite in our cities, which seem to have gone Mediterranean mad. And why not: the climate of most of our major cities suits Mediterranean living to a tee.

Like ceramic tiles, quarries and terracottas are cool underfoot, making them a good choice for the tropical or warm temperate climates. Some people like them in cooler climates too, and install underfloor heating for

those colder months of the year — a heavenly comfort.

Being unglazed, they are slightly porous. You can seal them to guard against stains in wet areas, but they also look attractive when they've worn down after a few years' wear and tear. Sealing can be a bit tricky, depending on the tile, but ask your tile manufacture, retailer or tradesperson — they'll put you on the right course.

Bricks

In the old days bricks, in all their different types, were probably a lot more common in domestic floors than they are today. Like terracotta and quarry tiles, brick can give that rustic country-style feel as well. Because of its heat absorption qualities, brick is good energy-efficient material, soaking up the sun all day then releasing it in the cool of the night.

Bricks give us the opportunity to make many varied patterns. There is the standard pattern that is used for walls, various basket weaves, herringbone, radial (circular) and 'stacked' where the bricks are placed in straight rows, forming a very simple pattern.

Although you can use normal house bricks for flooring if you like, the more common size is 'splits', so-called because they are split down the middle, thus giving the same surface area but half the thickness. There are various methods for laying flooring bricks but one thing you have to watch, as with all masonry and clay tiles, is the weight. The ideal subfloor, of course, is a concrete slab, but wood is fine provided it is strong and stable enough and properly sealed.

Masonry — marble, slate, terrazzo and concrete

Marble

Marble is usually associated with large public buildings such as churches, courts, town halls and office buildings but, nevertheless, you can create a real show-stopper of a floor with it at home, especially in entranceways and living rooms. A great idea, if you want to use it sparingly, is as a threshold, for example.

Although it looks and feels hard, marble is actually quite a porous stone — a kind of crystalline limestone — and is susceptible to stains and scratching unless it is sealed. Even then, sealing gives protection for a short time only and any spills need to be quickly wiped up. Marble can also get quite slippery when wet, so it is probably not the best material to use on kitchen and bathroom floors, although it can be absolutely stunning in the latter.

If you intend to use marble, check that the floor can carry the weight, or find a marble product — there are plenty available — such as thin tiles, marble chip tiles and veneers that will give you the effect without the massive weight.

Another plus is that cleaning it is extremely easy. Simply wipe over with diluted dishwashing liquid. Have a good talk to a professional about it, because if it's marble you want there's bound to be a product that will suit your needs.

Slate

Doorsteps, verandah edges, fireplace hearths, kitchen benchtops, billiard table tops — is there anywhere you can't use slate? With its gentle charcoals and warm red-browns, slate has a most elegant, yet informal character about it. It works just about everywhere in the house, most notably in hallways and kitchens.

Slate has some great natural qualities. For one, it is naturally laminated and is therefore resistant to scratching and stains, although the odd scratch, should it get one, merely seems to add to its character. It has good heat retention properties as well and so is recognised as a good choice in energy efficient houses.

Slate is usually supplied as square or rectangular tiles, although it can be bought in random shapes, like crazy paving as well. Just like any other tiles, it needs to be laid on a firm stable base to achieve the best result.

In Australia slate is generally available in three sizes with a natural split face finish and a diamond sawn edge: 300 mm x 300 mm, 605 mm x 300 mm and 605 mm x 605 mm. The thickness is approximately 15–20 mm. You can use the different sizes to form patterns, or just use one size. Slate can be used to give the effect of an old flagged floor. The tiles can be sealed to create a deeper gloss or left in their natural finish.

Terrazzo

Terrazzo is a beautiful, elegant flooring made of marble, granite or onyx chips in concrete resin and ground and polished to a smooth, semi-gloss finish. The concrete and resins can be plain or coloured to give a wider variety of effects. Terrazzo comes in slabs (heavy and expensive) and tiles. The slabs are normally used in commercial buildings while the tiles, laid like other tiles, are ideal for home.

Terrazzo is not cheap, but it has a fabulous array of advantages. It's non-slip, easily cleaned — just wipe over it with a mop and a little detergent diluted in warm water — and therefore requires minimal upkeep. It is very tough, won't stain or scratch and is pretty well impervious to household chemicals. But don't drop your tumbler of cordial on it; glass is no match for terrazzo.

Concrete

What would we do without the concrete slab? It's virtually revolutionised domestic flooring in the last 20 to 30 years, yet it is a centuries old mixture of cement powder, gravel, sand and water — one of the simplest and most cost-effective floors of all. Of course, it's mandatory in most high-rise buildings and apartments where it offers endless possibilities. Any surface at all — timber, floating floors, vinyl, terracotta tiles — can be laid over a concrete floor.

However, concrete itself need not be an interior decorator's nightmare. Hard wearing, long lasting, easily coloured, resistant to water and scratches and, if sealed, stains, concrete can be a genuine flooring alternative. It doesn't have to look like a footy stadium; in fact it can be made to work for you. So it is worth considering; if you're building a new house have the concrete slab finished so that you have to do nothing more.

There are various tricks to make a concrete floor more palatable. One is to expose some of the aggregate (the gravel) at the surface. This breaks the monotony of plain concrete and gives extra non-slip qualities. Colour is another consideration. Stains can be applied so a concrete floor can take on a number of different natural or colourful-looking alternatives. Then it can be sealed and polished. It can also be painted any colour you want using specialty paints to produce any of a myriad of colour possibilities. Once banished to the garden, concrete is now moving indoors and creating some great flooring alternatives.

WALLS AND CEILINGS

When I was small I had the annoying habit of writing on walls. They were a tempting canvas, just begging to be filled with drawings. I also had an imaginary friend called Poppy the Pixie, who used to be blamed for most of the naughty things I did.

One night my mother came in and immediately noticed a rather large addition to the graffiti already there. I even remember what it was — a girl's head with plaits that went on forever!

She went berserk, of course, having extracted many promises from me that I wouldn't do it again. It was Poppy the Pixie I shrieked, sensing that the game was probably up. Imagine my outrage when she whacked me and said, 'Well, give that to Poppy the Pixie next time you see him.'

My boys went through this stage as well but I got around it by letting them have a section of their own walls to decorate as they chose. And rather than wanting to hide their artworks, I quite like them. They're a wonderful record of their early childhood and are like a precious ancient wall mural.

When my older boy was in kindergarten he brought home his year's collection of paintings, which were gorgeous — rainbow colours in beautiful swirls and patterns. Rather than consign them to a cupboard, I glued them all onto a huge piece of wood panelling that we screwed to the wall to create a feature panel. It was absolutely stunning and Charlie was very proud that his artwork was on display.

choosing a look

Colours ➢ textures ➢ light ➢ spatial effects ➢ walls ➢ ceilings ➢ acrylics ➢ enamels ➢ washes ➢ glazes ➢ matt ➢ low sheen ➢ gloss ➢ paint effects ➢ wallpaper ➢ wood panelling

When you're setting out to redecorate a room, first decide on the 'look' or style you prefer. Do you want a colourful look, a subdued look, a natural look? Take into account any features such as the size of your room and whether it's a bright space or is short on natural light. Maybe there are pieces of furniture that determine the approach you take — you might have a baby grand piano, for instance, that is the centrepiece of your room, a beautiful antique fireplace, or a newly renovated floor. It's a good idea to work with these constraints, rather than against them. Of course, if you are renovating the entire room that's a different matter, but generally speaking it is a good idea to take into account any special features and work them into your overall plans.

One way to work out good solutions is to simply spend a lot of time in the room, looking and thinking it over — there's really no substitute for time in a home to work out what you really need. Do lots of research too. Get some magazines — there are always plenty to choose from at your local newsagent — visit your local library for books and journals, and check whether there is a trade advisory centre where you live.

It can be a great help, too, to get some professional advice. An interior decorator can really help you express and focus your ideas and make you aware of the pitfalls. And they can advise about the most economical ways of achieving your goals.

The most important thing is that you are able to achieve the look you had in mind, so that you're happy and content with the result.

painting

Painting is the simplest and most economical way of decorating the walls and ceiling of your home; and with the colours, textures and finishes available, the options are infinite. It is also something you can do yourself, making the job even cheaper, and with a little research, effort and skill can be every bit as good, if not better, than the quality of work you'd expect from a professional.

Painting can be a really cheap and effective way of making a statement with colour because it can be changed regularly at low cost unlike carpet, bathroom tiles and kitchen cabinets — if you don't like it, you can easily change it.

Let's start with the types of paints available.

Types of paints

Paint product	Type of paint	Used for
Wood primer	Oil and water-based sealant, provides a base for other coats to grip	Bare or exposed timber
Metal primer	Oil-based sealant, can also be rust inhibitor	Bare or exposed metal
Undercoat	Oil or acrylic based with good covering characteristics	On primed surfaces prior to top coat
Interior acrylic matt	Acrylic / water based	Lounge, dining, hallway, bedroom walls and ceilings, primed or bare timber furniture
Interior acrylic low sheen (satin)	Acrylic / water based	Satin sheen for walls and ceilings
Interior acrylic gloss	Acrylic / water based	Gloss sheen for furniture, windows, walls
Satin (semi-gloss) enamel	Oil-based enamel	Bathroom, kitchen and laundry walls, windows, doors, timber cupboards, furniture, metal
Gloss enamel	Oil-based enamel	Windows, doors, architraves, window frames, door frames, skirting, timber cupboards, furniture, metal
Woodstains	Oil / water based	Modifying the colour of woodwork
Wood wash		Bare timber lining boards, shelving, furniture, floors
Clear varnish	Oil / water based	Finishing natural, stained or stencilled woodwork
Tinted varnish — gloss, semi-gloss, matt	Oil / water based	Finishing natural woodwork
Polyurethane — gloss, semi-gloss, matt	Oil / water-based clear 'plastic' finish	Finishing natural, stained or stencilled woodwork
Lime wash	Lime and water based	Mediterranean-style for walls and ceilings
Milk paint	Water based	Chalky pastel finish for furniture

Planning painting

Painting is one of those jobs that you often put off doing around the home. If you plan ahead it will reduce the time the paint job takes dramatically. Points to consider are:

- The look you wish to create.
- Co-ordinating the colours with the rest of your furnishings and art work.
- Any problem areas that might need special attention.
- What sort of paint or finish do you need? Consider whether you need primer and what kind of paint or other coating you should use, whether you are thinking of using acrylic paint (water based) or enamel paint (solvent based).

Acrylic paints

Acrylic paints are available in finishes from flat to gloss. Because they are water thinned they are easier to use, especially when it comes to cleaning up the brush or roller. Soap and water are all that's needed. Being non-flammable and having a very mild odour, acrylic paints are ideal for interiors.

Water-based paints, of course, date back to when human beings first began decorating their dwellings. Usually called washes, they were made from lime, chalk and milk solids and coloured or tinted with various pigments. You could say that acrylic paint is modern technology's way of synthetically recreating old traditions.

Water-based acrylic paints have been used used worldwide, and their long-lasting performance is well proven.

The difference between water-based acrylic paint and solvent-based enamel paint is to do with the way they are formulated. Acrylic paints are formulated using resins that have a very different chemical composition than oil-based (enamel) paints.

Acrylic resins also dry by a different mechanism. The paint contains tiny spheres of polymers held in suspension in water. When it is applied to a surface, the water evaporates and the spheres are forced together by capillary pressure. With coalescents present to soften the surface, the spheres fuse together to form a continuous film of polymer. This is insoluble in water after the water and coalescents have evaporated.

Acrylics are alkali resistant and can be applied directly to alkali surfaces like fresh masonry, stucco and plaster.

Why use acrylic paints?

Acrylic paints were first used in Australia over twenty years ago and since then they have completely changed the way we paint our homes. Acrylic paints have proven to be both durable and economic to use. The major qualities that have made acrylic paints popular are:

- They are easy to use with a brush or roller.
- They are simple to clean up after painting because they are water based.
- They dry quickly — usually touch dry in 30 minutes — and are recoatable after 2 hours.
- Because acrylics are like a plastic film, the paint stretches and contracts with changes in weather and humidity and is less likely to crack.
- Acrylics allow water vapour out instead of blistering. On the other hand, acrylics are waterproof so water will not get in.
- Acrylics are available in a wide range of colours and finishes from flat to high gloss. Although the gloss finish is not as full gloss as an oil-based enamel, the gloss level is retained much better.

Most surfaces, if they have been properly prepared, can be painted with acrylics, i.e. brick, stone, fibro, masonry and timber. Acrylics are available in primers, undercoats and finishing coats for both exterior and interior use.

The attributes of acrylics are that they are mould resistant (although anything can go mouldy in some bathrooms), they have good adhesive qualities, low odour and are colour fast. In addition, they are non-yellowing and chalking is almost non-existent.

Acrylics may require a different approach to more conventional paints. For example, as they dry quickly it might be a good idea to have two brushes, one soaking in water that you change frequently. Use the other brush to paint with until it becomes dry, then swap brushes. Painting a hot, dry surface may have mixed results, so damp down the surfaces first before applying the paint. In very hot weather paint in the shade. Don't paint in very cold weather where the temperature is below 10°C.

Always read the manufacturer's label carefully and follow their instructions.

Enamel paints

Enamel paints are thinned with a solvent (usually turpentine) and are often used in areas where a large amount of cleaning is likely. Enamels are generally smoother and dry to a harder finish than acrylics. They are ideal in bathrooms and laundries, where it is constantly damp, or in children's bedrooms where frequent cleaning is needed because of grubby hands on the walls. Enamels can also be used outdoors for windows, screens, sills, shutters, walls, doors, fences and picnic tables.

Historians refer to oil paints dating back to sixteenth century England, although water-based paints such as distempers and lime washes were normally used at that time.

Modern enamel paints are not as easy to apply as acrylic paints, and need mineral turps for cleaning up. The odour is also much stronger during application than for acrylic paints and takes a few days to disperse.

Lime wash

The technique of using lime wash as a surface finish has been used for centuries and is still used as a traditional finish in places such as Tuscany in Italy, Provence in the south of France and Greece.

Recently there has been a trend, especially in the cities, towards painting walls with lime washes in the style of the traditional Mediterranean finishes. Lime wash can be used both inside and out and has become very popular where a weathered appearance is required. Lime wash paint creates a subtle mottled character like a 'bloom' that gives an aged 'soft' appearance. It can be applied to bare masonry and with the appropriate preparation it can also be painted over previously painted masonry, plasterboard, set plaster and most other wall surfaces — but not timber. It is difficult to match the colour if you need to patch up some spots; as with all specialist paint finishes, it's best to get advice from the supplier.

Caution with lime wash

Many people are unaware that once a lime wash has been applied, it is difficult to recoat using an acrylic or solvent-based paint. Lime wash may need to be professionally removed before the surface can be painted. If any trace of the lime wash remains it reacts and causes the paint to crack and peel within a short time.

Broken colour

Delicate broken colour has a subtle, marble-like finish. It is a two stage approach. First, you apply a low-sheen acrylic then, when dry, apply a special glaze. It can be ragged, rag rolled, dragged or sponged to produce a variety of painted effects. The low-sheen acrylic can be applied straight over existing matt or low-sheen paints, or over water-based undercoats. The glaze dries to a very low sheen, almost matt finish, and is fully washable. The glaze can be tinted and the end finish can be sealed with a clear sealer.

Distemper

Distemper is one of the simplest, most traditional interior paints. It is made by binding powdered chalk and pigments together that dry to a soft, velvet-like texture that is chalky in appearance. The paint dries to a thick opaque finish that gives a richness and depth to the colour used.

Milk paint

Milk paint is one of the most traditional finishes, popular in the eighteenth and ninteenth centuries on Shaker and country-style furniture as well as interior and exterior surfaces. Made from milk mixed with pigment to produce subtle mellow colours, milk paints were traditionally used to protect and decorate woods, achieving a soft mottled appearance.

No undercoat is necessary on new timber, as the first coat of milk paint acts as the undercoat on most softwoods and open-grained hardwoods. However, close-grained hardwood will need an initial coat of enamel primer or enamel undercoat. Check with your local supplier about how to best prepare the surface prior to starting the job.

Crackle medium

Crackle medium is a water-based and water-soluble finish for creating antique and decorative crackle effects on walls and furniture. The crackle medium is applied to the surface followed by the finishing coat.

When applying the finish, different types of brush strokes will create different cracks. Normal paint strokes will cause the top coat to split into linear cracks, while 'basketweave' strokes will cause cracks in all directions. If the wash is diluted with water the cracks will be much finer.

Primer

Prime coats of paint are needed for bare or new surfaces, or surfaces with areas where the paint has deteriorated. If an old layer of paint is not peeling or blistered it can be lightly sanded and serve as a prime coat. Check the can's label of the finish you have chosen because it will usually recommend an appropriate primer to use. Sometimes the final coat is also recommended for use as a primer.

Undercoat

An undercoat provides a base that the final coat will cover well. Undercoats need to have good adhesion, good filling capabilities and be quick drying. Most good undercoats can be used for both enamel and acrylic paints and can be used on previously painted enamel finishes provided they have been sanded. Always check the instructions on the can first.

Paint finish

Choosing between flat, gloss and satin

Generally paints are available in either gloss, satin or flat finishes.

- *Gloss or full gloss* is a shiny durable tough finish sometimes called full or high gloss.
- *Satin or semi-gloss* is halfway between gloss and flat and it can be called semi-gloss or low sheen.
- *Flat or matt* is non-reflective and is often termed as matt for this reason.

Practical reasons for selecting a particular paint finish might be to hide cracks or unevenness in a wall, so a flat paint might be chosen or a full gloss might be chosen because it will reflect light and brighten a room.

Generally home owners choose flat paints for living rooms and bedrooms and gloss for kitchens where a lot of cleaning and wiping is necessary. However, there are no hard and fast rules and paints are far more flexible than they were.

The amount of gloss in the paint indicates how hard wearing and durable the paint is. Generally gloss should last longer than satin and satin should last longer than flat paint. It is harder to scuff a hard-wearing enamel than a soft matt surface. And a higher gloss can withstand more cleaning and scrubbing without marking the finish.

The quality of a ceiling or wall surface will also influence the choice of finish. If a wall has been badly cracked and repaired a high gloss will show where the repairs have been made, whereas a matt finish will help to cover the repairs. Gloss finishes also enhance light reflections from down lighting and track lighting, creating interesting reflections in controlled lighting.

Ceilings

Bedroom, hall, lounge and dining room ceilings are usually painted with a flat finish. They are not likely to be scuffed or even scrubbed and so flat finishes are ideal. For ceilings in kitchens, bathrooms and laundries, where cooking odours and steam accumulates, you may need to use a gloss or semi-gloss. For maximum 'scrubbability' use a full gloss.

Many people regard painting ceilings as a difficult and messy job — however careful they are there always seems to be a slow dribble of paint off the brush onto their hands, or it literally 'rains' all over them and the floor. Paint manufacturers have developed non-drip paints that solve this problem. Non-drip paints are slightly different to conventional paints; the most important thing to remember is don't stir the paint or it will lose its non-drip properties. After tinting or shaking the paint needs to stand for at least four hours to regain its non-drip characteristics.

When removing the lid from the can there may be a brownish or clear liquid on the surface of the paint. Do not try to mix it in. Non-drip paint clings to the brush, so you will need to dip it differently too. Dunk the brush straight into the paint and the correct amount will remain on the brush. There is no need to wipe off excess paint on the edge of the can as this will reduce the paint's non-drip characteristics.

You paint the ceiling in the normal way, applying the paint as you would any other paint. The difference will be that the paint will not drip, splatter or run like normal paint, although it is still recommended to use drop sheets in case of accidents. Non-drip paints are available in a wide choice of colours and finishes and are available as solvent based or water based. Some vinyl paints even have their own tray; simply peel off the lid and it is ready to use.

NONI SAYS

Wash walls and ceilings with a mild detergent and water before painting so dust and dirt doesn't discolour the paint.

Tips for painting ceilings

- If using acrylic paints use a brush to paint a strip around the corners of the ceiling, then fill in the centre with a roller. Using a paint roller for the body of the ceiling will save time and eliminate the need to stand on ladders for long periods.
- If using enamel paint, work across a narrow area of the ceiling. Start in a corner and paint a narrow strip of the same width, working from the unpainted area into the still wet area. This will eliminate any lap marks that may appear. When you get to areas near the wall, a brush and a paint guard will make a smooth finish to the painted surface.

Walls

Walls generally need only a flat finish except for kitchens, bathrooms and laundries. But if you have young children a semi-gloss may be more appropriate. Gloss paint in bathrooms and laundries copes best with the effects of steam and condensation.

Woodwork

In most cases the use of a semi-gloss or high-gloss paint is recommended, because they are more durable, can be wiped over and they repel water better. You could even use a tinted colour on the wood trim to complement the wall colour. If the grain quality is good and there are no unsightly blemishes in the wood, try using a clear polyurethane finish to enhance the grain and give the natural look very popular nowadays.

Colour

The psychology of colours should be regarded as a guide rather than a rule; however, they are something to keep in mind when decorating.

- Yellows, oranges, reds are warm colours.
- Green, blues and purples are cool colours.
- Light colours such as white and yellow are airy, expansive and cheerful.
- Dark colours such as navy blue or brown can create a cosy, sophisticated feeling.

Colour

Consider the 'temperature effect' of a colour if you want to 'warm up' a room on the shady side of a house or 'cool off' a room on the sunny side.

Use light colours in small, dark areas that you want to look larger and brighter. Use dark colours in an overly large room.

The 'rules' regarding colours apply throughout the home. Dark, sombre colours such as blues and browns may make the room feel restful, even classical, but they may also create a closed-in effect if the room is small. Yellow can make a room feel expansive and cheerful, but it can also affect the restfulness of the room. Red and orange can make a bold statement, but it can be confronting. Generally speaking, green is the closest colour to nature and has a refreshing and calming effect, that is, if it is not too dark and sombre.

One of the first things to take into account with choosing colours for walls or ceilings is the amount of natural light in the room. If your room relies mainly on artificial lighting, make sure the colours you choose don't 'change colour' under your house lights. Yellows can be particularly susceptible, turning either cooler or warmer depending on the light.

A painted ceiling is a refreshing way to perk up a dull room. You can emphasise a colour and motif found in the room or use a contrasting colour to attract the eye. For a small room paint the ceiling a light colour to give the feeling of space or, if the room has coloured walls, try a lighter shade of the wall colour. And a ceiling painted with a high-gloss enamel will reflect light where there is little or no natural light. Colours can be used to create various illusions such as bringing a feature wall forward or make it appear further away. These are great effects to use if your room feels too big or too small. By using washes you can graduate the colour of a wall to slightly lighter as it reaches the ceiling. This creates the effect of a higher ceiling, especially if the ceiling is painted in a light colour.

There are a whole range of techniques that can be used to decorate ceilings using designs. One way is to stencil a pattern around the edge of the ceiling. Even one large stencil, like a ceiling rose, in the middle of the ceiling can look very attractive and can reflect colours already used in the room or its furnishings.

Another idea is to paint several closely spaced borders of colour in graduating tones or contrasting hues. This can give a formal feel to a rather ordinary room.

Stencils

The use of stencils on walls is another decorating idea that can be very effective — even the simplest pattern. Try picking up the colour of something else in the room in your stencil, such as a colour in the carpets or curtains.

Stencils are not hard to do, the simplest being very basic shapes like a square or triangle, or you can get a little more sophisticated. First, using a length of tracing paper or lightweight drawing paper, design and draw the stencil using a soft pencil such as a 2B or 4B. You can use all sorts of things as your inspiration — designs in ceramic tiles are good, material designs are another. Then pin the paper to a lightweight piece of cardboard and trace over your design to transfer it onto the card. Cut out the design with a blade, then mark a faint line along the wall to act as a guide or level for the stencil, usually just below the ceiling. Place the stencil level with the faint line, and with an artist's brush paint over the stencil. The choice of paint for your stencil depends on the background surface, however, acrylic paint usually does the job. A stencil can either be a contrasting colour or a shade matching the background. Repeat the stencil following the faint line you have drawn.

Kitchens — the heart and soul of the home

When I was small, a family friend who I called Auntie Helen had the most wonderful kitchen. A visit to Auntie Helen's house meant one thing — a big feed.

She had shelves decorated with newspaper cut with decorative edges that were stacked with richly coloured preserved fruit, a freezer bulging with shallow metal trays of homemade ice-cream and a fuel stove that always had a big pot of something yummy bubbling away.

I remember her collection of brightly coloured aprons and the vivid hues of various sized tins that held a vast assortment of homemade cakes and biscuits. There were soft yellow bakelite canisters with pale green lids, a huge metal teapot and a painted wooden cabinet with frosted glass panels in the doors that held china, glasses, cutlery, tea towels and napkins.

It's no wonder that these homely kitchens of the past have enjoyed a revival. The so-called 'country' kitchen represents nurturing and sustenance, a room where people come first. At the other end of the spectrum is the trend towards sleek, minimalist kitchens where everything is hidden away behind cupboards and in drawers. In fact, some new city apartments don't even have kitchens, because the people who live in them don't want to cook.

Whatever your taste, the advances in technology and design make it possible to incorporate today's terrific storage and shelving concepts and labour-saving appliances into almost any style.

Painting is the simplest and most economical way of decorating the walls and ceiling of your home; and with the colours, textures and finishes available, the options are infinite. It is also something you can do yourself, making the job even cheaper, and with a little research, effort and skill can be every bit as good, if not better, than the quality of work you'd expect from a professional.

The most common paint finishes used for kitchen ceilings and walls are low-sheen washable acrylics and semi-gloss enamels. Many of us like to make the kitchen bright and colourful, so it is a room that gives us the opportunity to play with different matching or contrasting colours and textures.

Kitchens often have a number of prefinished areas such as benches, cupboards and tiled walls at the work areas (see Surfaces, finishes and precious things page 205). However, even just concentrating on the walls and ceilings, there are still plenty of painting options open to us.

As the kitchen is the room everyone spends the most time in, most people probably know what they would most like. For instance, a kitchen might be too dark and need to have a lighter and more spacious look; you may want it to be the 'bright spot' of your home — cheerful and friendly; you may live in a rural setting and it may adjoin the garden, and you would like it to be more connected to the garden.

It's a good idea to check out the effect of your lighting on the colours you have in mind. Even if you're going to employ a painting contractor to do the job, it's good to know that the colours are going to work. Do a few test boards so you can see how the daylight and artificial lights affect the colours — these work better than swatches, which are printed with ink rather than the actual paint.

Have a think, too, about the different textures and patterns you can use. There are great opportunities in the kitchen for patterns and stencils. If you are having trouble choosing from the array of choices, sometimes choosing a theme such as Tuscan or Provencal, 1950s or country style can make it easier.

Bathrooms

Years of heavy use can take away the fresh atmosphere that is so pleasant in a bathroom, but a new coat of paint can work wonders.

Due to the humid atmosphere in most bathrooms the type of paint used is very important. It is best to purchase paints that are low sheen, semi-gloss or full gloss to ensure durability in the wettest room in the house!

Bathroom walls and ceilings have to stand up to a lot of dampness with water and steam, which is why mould is often a problem. Mould is a living plant organism that is scattered by air currents or insect movements. To be able to prosper on walls and ceilings the mould or mildew spores need food and moisture, which is generally present in bathrooms in the form of dust, dirt, water and steam.

Bathrooms and laundries often lack ventilation and have an excess of moisture, the main causes of mould growth. Damage can be costly if mould is left to take a grip on painted surfaces, but it is simple enough to remove for repainting.

First, wash with a brush or sponge, using a solution of one cup of household bleach to nine cups of water. Allow the solution to stay on the surface for a least 10 minutes before rinsing it off thoroughly with clean water. In very bad cases, two or more washings with the bleach solution may be necessary.

Allow the surface to dry completely and then, as an

added protection, you may like to apply an anti-mould solution, available at most paint and hardware stores. When it is dry, paint the surface in the usual manner without washing off the anti-mould solution. You may also like to take the added step of having a fungicidal additive mixed into the paint. This service is available from good paint stockists.

The bathroom may not be large in comparison to other rooms in the home, but as it is not a room where people spend a lot of time, you can be more adventurous with your colour choices. Dramatic or subtle, any colour choice or combination can brighten up a bathroom.

In choosing colours you should also consider the existing bathroom fixtures such as baths, basins and, of course, tiles. By repainting walls and ceiling and perhaps, by purchasing new hand and face towels, your bathroom can be dramatically transformed. If you want the room to look larger, use a light colour on the walls and the wood trims. The ceiling can be a different colour, perhaps a light tint in a contrasting or complementary colour.

Remember, in bathrooms careful consideration must be given to the type of paint, colour, proper surface preparation and application methods. It is only after the effective employment of all four that you will be assured the best results.

Tips for countering mould in bathrooms

- Choose the correct paint — read the can carefully and ask for advice from your supplier.
- Give extra consideration to air circulation and extraction. In some bathrooms, it isn't enough to open a window before showering, though it is better than nothing. A wall, ceiling or window extractor fan will help preserve your hard work.

The kids' rooms

Children use their rooms as a great source of expression and something they can call their own. Decorating their bedrooms with different coloured toys, hangings and curtains can be a primary source of inspiration to young developing minds.

The vitality of your children's bedrooms can be greatly enhanced by highlighting all the existing colours with a fresh coat of paint as a background to the existing colour tones. You can choose fresh wall and ceiling colours to co-ordinate with the present colours utilised in their furnishings. Young children like bright colours such as blue, green and red and many furnishings for this age group contain a mix of these colours in their designs. Primary colours have traditionally been considered most appropriate for toddlers, but sometimes these colours can be very aggressive.

The size of the room is another important factor to be considered when planning a new wall colour. With small rooms, light shades or indeed white with bright trim work will give the illusion of larger spaces. For teenagers, girls may opt for mid tones or pastel colours. Boys may prefer stronger combinations.

Paint selection is another important aspect of painting children's rooms. These days, paints are available in both gloss or low gloss washable finishes, which will make the job of removing grubby marks much easier. A coat of paint will enrich the mood of any room, no more so than your children's bedroom. Colour stimulates the imagination and can help create an environment that will help your children grow and develop.

How much paint will be needed?

Normal coverage will give you roughly 16 square metres to the litre, depending on the texture and how absorbent the surface is.

To calculate the surface area, measure the height and width of each area and multiply to find the number of square metres of surface. Don't forget to allow for any doors and windows. The label on the paint will tell you the exact number of square metres that a litre of paint will cover. Divide that into the number of square metres to obtain the number of litres per coat to buy.

It's always a good idea and a wise investment to choose good quality paint applicators. This will produce a more satisfying result and a better looking job. Here is a list of the common applicators.

Brushes

NONI SAYS

To keep paint off window glass while you are painting, use a card to protect the frame and apply a thin coat of vaseline to the glass 2–4 centimetres out from the edge of the frame. Paint the frame as carefully as you can and let the paint dry. Any paint that strayed onto the glass should come off easily.

- Natural long bristle brushes are suitable for acrylics and water-based paints. Good quality paint brushes that are fuller in bristle, allowing the flow of paint from the brush to be smoother, which gives an even finish, are best for areas such as walls and ceilings.
- Natural short bristle brushes are recommended for gloss enamels and polyurethane plastic paints. This brush is best for doors, window frames etc. as it can be controlled better than a long bristle brush. It should be thicker, yet full in bristle.
- Synthetic bristle brushes can be used for acrylics and water-based paints. They are suited to rough work such as brickwork and cement render where a tough bristle is required. Pure natural bristle brushes will wear away quickly if used for this work.
- There are also different brushes for different jobs — sash cutters are used for painting edgings and fitches are small brushes designed for detailed work.

Never allow the brush the chance to dry out after you have finished painting. Soak the brush in the recommended solvent, then wash in warm soapy water with either a soap bar or mild detergent. Finally, rinse in cold water and comb natural bristle brushes straight with an old comb.

A brush is not always the best answer; there are all sorts of applicators for applying paint, so it's a good idea to check out what is available for different types of jobs.

Applicators

- Painting pads are fast and easy to use with less splattering than rollers. They are available in many sizes and shapes. Check with your paint store to see the range that is available and to see if a paint pad is suitable for your particular job.

- Rollers: lambswool rollers are best for matt acrylics, while orlon is used for gloss and semi-gloss acrylics. Mohair and foam rubber rollers are used for gloss and semi-gloss enamels on surfaces such as doors, and polyester is more suitable for rougher surfaces. Rollers are easy to use and can be put on long poles for painting ceilings. You can get little rollers, too, for doing detail work.
- Spray guns are ideal for furniture.
- Aerosol spray packs are also available in many paint types and colours. They are best for smaller jobs.

Choosing the right applicator will save you time and money and give a better result.

Surface preparation

When painting walls or ceilings, try following these steps for preparing your surfaces:

- Examine walls and ceilings for cracks or blemishes and fill small hairline cracks with spackling material. Fill larger cracks with special patching plaster.
- Sand lightly when dry for a smooth surface.
- Clean the surface to remove dust, oil, grease, rust and flaking paint.
- Remove all hardware from doors and windows and loosen light fixtures or cover these areas with masking tape and scraps of paper or cloth.

Spending time preparing the surface before you paint will save you a lot of work in the long run. There is nothing more frustrating than to paint a room and then find that poor preparation has caused the paint to lift or that cracks have been overlooked.

If you are not too steady up a ladder, then attach the long handle of a broom to the end of a roller so you can reach those high spots. You may still need to stand on a table but it is not as scary as a ladder.

Cleaning and caring for freshly painted walls and woodwork

Take care of your newly painted surfaces with regular cleaning. For normal everyday stains use a mild detergent in warm water on a soft cloth, rubbing in a gentle circular motion. It is sometimes better if a little detergent is dabbed onto the stain and left to work for a while, then washed off.

With ingrained scuffs such as those caused by a box or furniture bumping the walls — or ballpoint pens, marking pens or blue tak, which are more difficult to remove — a spray cleanser may be used. These should be sprayed on and left to work for a while, before being rinsed clean using fresh water. It is always better to wash a much larger area than the stain so the surface doesn't become over polished.

Gloss finishes may be wiped with non-abrasive cleaners as frequently as necessary.

Rubbing hand cream on your hands and arms before painting can make paint removal much easier.

Spilt paint

No matter how much care we take in protecting floors, furniture and other objects, inevitably some paint splatters onto areas that it shouldn't. The secret in removing spots and spills is to get to work on them before they dry and become impossible to remove, especially from carpet. As soon as a spill occurs, scrape up the surface paint then soak up as much of what is left as you possibly can.

If the spilt paint is water based, repeatedly rinse the area with water until the area is clean. Soak up the water with a clean sponge. If the paint is enamel based, massage and sponge the remaining paint with mineral turpentine. If it is in the carpet speed is of the essence. Make sure that the area is thoroughly washed as soon as possible after the spill for the best chance of minimising the effects.

Green tip

You can look after our environment by disposing of paint in two ways:

- Get rid of leftover paint by pouring it onto an absorbent material such as kitty litter, cardboard, rags or shredded paper and allow to dry. Once the paint is dry it can be disposed of with your normal household garbage. If you allow the empty can to dry out thoroughly, it can also be disposed of with your normal household garbage.
- Contact your local council for guidelines on the disposal of any quantity of liquid paint.

Before you start to paint wrap some clingwrap around the paint can and put it on a sheet of newspaper. The clingwrap and newspaper will catch all the runs as you paint. When you finish, discard the clingwrap and newspaper and you will be left with a nice clean paint can ready to be put away.

Lead in paint: what you need to know

It is rare these days for paint to contain lead. The maximum permissible lead content in household paints is 0.25 per cent.

Some types of paint, particularly old gloss paint found mainly on metalwork and in old buildings, may contain lead as a pigment. It becomes a health hazard when it is disturbed by sanding or scraping. Please don't disturb paint that you think may contain lead. There are important health and environmental guidelines to follow in its removal. If you encounter old paint and think that it may contain lead, you can buy a lead test kit from hardware shops and also from some major paint manufacturers or distributors.

If the surface is good and common sense tells you it is not posing a threat to health, you can simply paint over it, thereby sealing it in. Alternatively, you may decide that the paint should be removed. These sorts of jobs can be very dangerous to your health and you should contact a professional.

Painting tips

- Stirring: paint is stirred so that the pigments and ingredients are evenly mixed throughout, which gives the paint a consistent finish. Use a long flat stirrer and stir from bottom to top using semi-circular strokes. Continue stirring until the paint flows freely. Stir again while painting, especially if you have to leave the paint unused for any period of time. Use a paddle attached to an electric drill if there is a lot of stirring to be done.
- Skin: a skin can form on acrylic paints when an open can of paint is left for some time. The skin needs to be removed and discarded. To do this, cut the skin around the edges of the can using a knife, then wrap it in newspaper and discard.

Solving painting problems

Here are the most common problems, their causes and how to rectify them.

- Bleeding occurs when soluble extracts in wood penetrate through the new coating and stain it. A primer is needed to prevent the stain bleeding before applying the final finish.
- Cracking can be caused by moisture under the paint, coatings that are dry and inflexible under the new paint, poor mixing of the paint and uneven application of the paint. To solve the problem, remove the cracked paint and any underlying coatings. This can be done with sandpaper or you may consider using a hot air paint stripper, which can remove several layers of paint easily. Use a scraper to remove the softened paint. Do not repaint until the surface is dry.
- Cross-grain cracking: this problem is often caused by too many layers of paint that have become hard and unable to expand along with the wood surface. Remove the layers of paint as above and repaint.
- Flaking occurs when paint has been applied to either a moist or excessively hot surface, where an inferior coating has been used, or where the application has been uneven. The paint needs to be removed and repainted. Choose the correct quality paint and make sure the surface is completely dry and paint in a cool part of the day.
- Peeling, where large pieces lift off from a previously coated surface. This is usually caused by water under the paint surface, or painting over a surface that is too hard, smooth, glossy or chalky for the paint to adhere to. Remove the paint and allow the surface to dry before repainting. Hard, smooth or glossy surfaces should be rubbed with glasspaper to provide a rougher surface for the new paint to adhere to.

Use a sheet of clingwrap to cover the paint tin while you go and make a cup of tea or have to do something other than painting, so the paint doesn't dry out.

- Chalking is where whitish chalky patches appear on the paint surface, usually because the paint is old or badly weathered. Remove the chalking by brushing vigorously and washing. Repaint in the usual manner.
- Poor surface preparation causes problems such as peeling paint, rusted metal or damaged masonry. Properly preparing surfaces for painting will eliminate many problems.

Wallpaper

Wallpaper is a grand old form of wall decorating that has been around for centuries and, except for some minor modifications due to technological advances, little has changed in the way wallpapering is carried out today. Looking back, we can suppose that wallpapering had its roots with early cave dwellers who painted 'stories', familiar images and stencilled shapes on their rough walls. However, it wasn't until the advent of cheap, continuous paper rolls and mass printing techniques that wallpapering became a popular form of wall decoration. Wallpapering can give a sense of great formality to a room, even a certain grandeur. Alternatively, there are lots of fun designs about these days — try the Elvis wallpaper — that can give your room a very unique personality indeed.

Wallpaper can be used on any type of wall in any room of the home and can be applied using a number of different approaches. For example, it can run from ceiling to floor, or from the top of the skirting board to the dado rail at about 900 mm high, or as a border of co-ordinating wallpaper about 100 mm wide, replacing the dado rail. Some papers are available as a pair of co-ordinating papers and a border — the second can be applied above the dado rail or to a different wall.

Wallpapers are available in rolls of various lengths and widths — the most usual are from 6 metres to 30 metres in length and 75 cm, 90 cm and 130 cm in width. There are lots of different colours, types and textures, of course, including:

- Lining: used under the final or finished wallpaper to smooth out rough or cracked walls.
- Flock: a raised pattern that looks like velvet.
- Embossed: a raised pattern.
- Grassweave: applied to a paper backing — no match is required.
- Wall vinyl: often an American product with a width of 54 inches (137 cm) and fabric backing, impact resistant and scrubbable. Good for high traffic areas.
- Paint imitations: these papers imitate paint finishes and can be finished in wax and polished with a woollen cloth.
- Textile: silk or linen-faced papers with a paper backing.
- Fibreglass: can be fixed to walls and painted over.

If you have the time and the inclination, wallpapering can be a rewarding do-it-yourself project. But talk to the experts first.

Tips on cleaning wallpaper

- Ordinary 'unfinished' wallpaper: be very cautious when cleaning wallpapers that have no vinyl finish as the surface can be easily damaged. As well, the colours may run and, if it is dampened, the wallpaper may loosen from the wall.
- Always try dusting first using a duster especially kept for the purpose, a soft brush (covered with a soft cloth) or a soft brush attachment on your vacuum cleaner.
- For hard-to-remove marks first assess what they are and cautiously use an appropriate process. For example, many people suggest simple solutions such as gently rubbing marks with an art gum or pencil eraser.
- Vinyl or washable surfaces: use a soft tightly wrung out cloth that has been dipped in a mild detergent solution. Some tougher vinyl finishes will allow stronger rubbing and harsher cleansers. Consult your retailer or manufacturer.

Wall tiles

After painting, tiling is probably the most popular way of decorating walls, and there is literally a world of ceramic tiles in all sorts of colours, designs, textures and sizes to suit any need. Ceramic tiles have been around for centuries — the Persian, Roman, Spanish and Italian societies have all been great fans of tilework. They are made from clay that is glazed and fired at very high temperatures. Some tiles with special patterns may be fired a number of times, once for each design element or colour.

One of the great things about wall tiles is the variety available. They range from classical or plain styles in simple whites and pastel colours, deeper colours such as rich blues and greens and ochres, to intricate reliefs and friezes and hand-painted styles. And, just to add to the variety, there are glass, marble and natural stone tiles as well.

Tiles come in lots of different sizes. There are standard-sized tiles that measure about 150 mm x 150 mm and 200 mm x 200 mm; there are tiny little glass (or mosaic) tiles that are about 20 mm x 20 mm; and there are pencil thin tiles, border and dado tiles, picture and relief (or textured) tiles, feature tiles, insert tiles and hand-crafted ones as well. They are available in an enormous range of colours, designs and patterns.

With such a range to choose from the best approach is to first decide on the colours that appeal to you and begin to look at what is available in those shades you like. If you can picture your ideas in your mind it's a safe bet there will be tiles available for what you want to do.

When you're choosing tiles make sure you insist on being able to lay the samples out as you want them in the shop before you make a final decision. One shop I went to had the feature trim tiles at one end of the shop hung on cards and the main wall tiles at the other. I had to make quite a fuss to get them put together, but it was worth it. It doesn't matter what they say about you when you've left the shop it's essential that you're happy with your choices, especially if mistakes are going to prove inconvenient and costly.

Choosing wall tiles

Take a good look around the room you want to tile. Ask yourself some questions.

Question 1: Is tiling the best solution?

Tiling is a great wall finish in kitchens, bathrooms and laundries. For bedrooms, lounge rooms, dining rooms, hallways and entranceways it can also be the perfect solution in certain types of homes, but there are other factors to consider. Tiles are more expensive than other wall finishes, but on the other hand maintenance is negligible and 40 years later the tiles can still be in perfect condition and looking great. It's not a good idea to change your mind after you've tiled a wall — it's a big job to rip them all off again. So the answer is, take your time, don't rush it.

Question 2: What is the main purpose of the tiles — functional or decorative feature?

Functional areas are kitchens, bathrooms and laundries; generally speaking, areas where tiles are more of a decorative feature are lounge rooms, dining rooms, hallways and entranceways and bedrooms. For functional areas you want an easy-to-clean surface without too much texture unless a non-slip surface is important. Patterns may be a good idea in places like the kitchen so food marks do not show up so easily (handy with youngsters about). Alternatively, you may like a very plain surface

that gives you that spotless look. For decorative areas cleaning is not such an issue as regular dusting with the occasional wipe over with a damp cloth normally does the trick.

Question 3: How should the tiling look?

Try visualising it. Consider issues such as space, light and function. As with any wall finish, tiles can have a great influence on the lightness and spatial look of your room. White tiles will generally make your room look bigger and, because white reflects light well, you'll find there'll be less reliance on artificial light than with darker and more sombre colours. Big expanses of white tiles can look very plain, 'clinical' and minimalist. That may be the look you want; however, it may be that you need to add some colour such as a border or frieze. Borders are an edging often at the bottom or top of the tiled area, whereas friezes are commonly at waist or picture rail height. Random tiles — illustrated, painted or simply of a different colour — can look very effective too.

Question 4: How do I know I've made the right decision?

A good way to confirm your ideas and get new and better ideas is research — buy some home-maker magazines that feature wall tiles or architectural magazines, which are usually available from better newsagents. Take a browse in your local bookshop for the latest home decorator books. Visit friends. Check out your library. Visit manufacturers and retail tile outlets. Some cities have building information centres that you can visit to see all the latest materials available. And if you're still in a quandary, consult a qualified interior decorator.

Types of tiles

Standard: The standard wall tile, usually plain or patterned in a simple motif, comes in many colours, patterns and sizes. They are usually square in shape, but rectangular and other shapes are available too. Larger tiles often work better on large expanses of wall, which can sometimes look too busy if small tiles are used. Smaller tiles tend to work better in small areas such as splashbacks above kitchen sinks.

Mosaic (glass): These are small ceramic tiles measuring about 20 mm x 20 mm. They were once called 'glass tiles' because they were often made of mineral and glass. Because of their tiny size, mosaics are ideal for curved surfaces. They are available in sheet form where a number of tiles are attached to a backing sheet or front sheet and can be laid in sections, which takes a lot of the work out of it. However, laying them evenly is a difficult job for the do-it-yourselfer.

Hand-painted: These are great fun — and you know, well you hope, that you've got something unique. Hand-painted tiles come in illustrations and motifs and make great friezes. Sometimes you can find a series of tiles that make up an ongoing picture or motif pattern.

Borders and friezes: There's a great range of tiling solutions available in borders and friezes. Dream up one; you'll probably find it's available. Borders and friezes are mostly rectangular in shape and range from pencil thin through patterned, textured, textured relief and pictures. And the colour range is amazing.

Inserts: As the name implies, these are small, usually plain-coloured tiles that are used, for example, to break up a large expanse of colour on a wall. They fit into the corner where four tiles meet; standard tiles with one corner missing can be purchased to fit the insert.

Colour and design influences

As we make decisions on decorating our homes we continually come across a word that is used in several different ways: 'style'. Sometimes it infers 'stylish', but often it refers to a design influence. Sometimes, considering the different design styles can be very helpful in deciding how to use wall tiles in your home.

Strong, dynamic colours can make a great statement. Imagine a bathroom or kitchen: you enter and are confronted by the various pieces of furniture and fixtures and four walls of rich, blue mosaic tiles. It certainly lets you know you're in the room! Another solution could be a feature wall of strong, vibrant dynamic colours, either in a pattern or in random form. One piece of advice if you're using strong and dynamic colours: use a design that will be lasting and won't go out of date. It'll drive you crazy if it does.

White backgrounds with blue patterns are an old favourite with wall tile designs. It is very much the classical approach where vast expanses of white tiles are broken with borders and friezes of royal or navy blue. They might be a narrow line of tiny mosaics laid to make a chequerboard pattern, or two rows of standard-sized blue tiles but laid in an ongoing pattern amongst the background white tiles. Then there are patterned tiles, often rectangular in shape, which can make a great frieze. Other colours can be used for the classical look too: try dark greens, reds and red-ochre colours.

Just about every magazine on home decorating features a country look; in fact there are whole magazines devoted to what has become a very recognisable design style. Here is the opportunity for the rustic look using wall tiles of natural colours or slightly antique whites that work with natural timber colours so often present in country-style kitchens or bathrooms. Take the opportunity to invent feature 'panels' and friezes of flowers, fruits and vegetables and country scenes. Hand-painted tiles are a real plus in country-style designs.

The modern look is probably epitomised by black and white and stainless steel. Walls decorated in all whites, all blacks and combinations of both can look anything from classical to futuristic. The all-white minimalist bathroom, with it's large glass frameless shower room and sleek appointments, has become a feature of homes worldwide — the global bathroom. So has the black kitchen, with its black venetian blinds, black feature walls behind black or stainless steel cooktops and refrigerators — it's a great ultra-modern look. Also utterly stylish are plays on black and white: white-tiled walls with black trim and vice versa, played off against black and white marble floors, furniture and fixtures.

Wall tiling is a quite manageable do-it-yourself job, but it does take time, patience and some fairly meticulous work if you want to make it look good. Your job will be made a lot easier if you have the right tools, make a plan of your design, prepare the surface properly and follow the directions of the various products you use. Don't be afraid to get professional advice, because every little bit will make your job easier and more successful in the end.

Timber
wall panelling

Decorative timber wall panelling can provide a feature in the family home. Matching a mood, creating an ambience, attracting attention — whatever the need, timber panelling can be eye-catching.

Selecting timber panelling from the dozens of alternatives needs some careful consideration — availability, wear resistance, hardness, colours, grain, patterns, method of fixing, appropriate fittings and finishes and, of course, cost.

Solid timber panelling is readily available from local timber merchants where you have a choice of several popular species and machined profiles or styles. Popular species are radiata pine, western red cedar, Pacific maple, various oaks and oregon, but specialty suppliers and merchants may be able to offer a more extensive range.

Australian woodpanelling species

Brush box, spotted gum, various messmates (stringybark), jarrah, karri, tallowwood, blackbutt, alpine ash, Tasmanian oak, New England oak, cypress pine, radiata pine, hoop pine, slash pine, Tasmanian myrtle, poplar, celery-top pine, blackwood, Queensland kauri pine, silky oak and more!

Foreign woodpanelling species available in Australia

Western hemlock (Canada pine), teak, belau, rimu, Baltic pine, merbau (kwila), various oaks, Californian redwood, Chilean alerce, Nordic white fir, matai, silver ash to name but a few.

The cost of wall panelling varies depending on thickness, width, quality, scarcity of the species, profile, cutting loss (wastage), random or set lengths, fixing and finishing. As a general rule, the lowest cost materials are those most readily available such as plantation pine. And unless you are an ardent do-it-yourselfer, wall panelling is best installed by an expert, so cost should be taken into account as well.

Just as timber patterns can dictate mood and the texture of the panelling can enhance calm and comfort, so too can a pattern affect the visual unity, flow and rhythm of a room. Patterns can also alter the spatial feel, and profiled timber panelling can be readily utilised to this end by fixing it in various patterns — vertical, horizontal or angled.

By vertically installing profiled panelling, rooms with low ceilings can seem taller; similarly, panelling installed horizontally can make a room seem wider. A herringbone pattern can point upwards to 'lift' the eye or downwards to create the illusion of a lower ceiling, while a diagonal pattern can provide a kind of 'informality' to a square-shaped wall. Alternatively, to create a more formal effect, use panelling on only the upper or lower section of the wall. It can look great.

Of course, there are other mood-altering options such as colour and grain (including stains) and width and profile. Certain panelling can have a dampening effect on sound as well.

Timber wall panelling can be fixed in any number of ways:

- Nailing: driven through the face, heads punched below the surface, holes filled with putty.
- Concealed nailing: generally used for narrower boards where the nail head is covered by the overlap of the adjoining panel.
- Adhesive: make sure you consult an expert when using adhesive on wall boards.
- Clip-on: some products feature clip-on mounting. Some systems allow for relatively simple demounting of the panelling as well.
- Screws: occasionally appropriate but seldom used because of the difficulty of concealing the heads.

Various government and local authorities have different regulations relating to timber panelling. These often relate to certain areas within non-domestic buildings such as assembly areas, escape corridors, lift foyers and theatres. Just make sure to discuss it with a professional or your local authority.

Typical finishing processes involve sanding the faces smooth and clear finishing with varnishes, clear polyurethane-type finishes, Scandinavian oil or clear water-thinnable acrylic or polyurethane finishes. For a guide to the effect of a finish on the final colour of the panelling, try swabbing a spare panel or test area with mineral turpentine — it should give you a pretty good indication while the turpentine is wet.

Timber wall panelling with its huge range of widths, profiles, species, grains, colours, patterns and finishes provides a marvellous palette for the home decorator. Creating a good-looking, livable interior requires a little imagination, a bit of research and sometimes a professional eye. Never be shy about getting help from your local expert.

Tips on cleaning timber panelling

- Dust regularly with a duster, soft cloth, soft long-handle brush or broom, or using a soft brush attachment on your vacuum cleaner.
- Sealed panelling: never wet the panelling; rather, used a tightly wrung out cloth that has been dipped in a light detergent solution. Finish by using a cloth dampened by water only, then use another cloth to dry. There are all-purpose household cleaners that will also assist with cleaning. Ask your local handyperson centre or hardware store for the most suitable product.
- Sealed panelling: dust regularly and re-wax as necessary. If the wax has built up to a degree that makes cleaning difficult, try using white spirit or a wax cleaning product to remove the built up wax, then refinish.
- Old and tarnished waxed panelling: consult a local expert on this one, though gently rubbing down with a fine steel wool and white spirit can often bring the surface back to an excellent condition.

Timber wall panelling in bathrooms and laundries

If you have timber wall panelling as a feature throughout your home, you may want to continue it into the more humid rooms such as the bathroom and laundry. Because humid and wet environments can affect timber, there are a number of precautions worth taking.

- Ventilation: the most important thing is to ensure there is good ventilation. A well-ventilated room protects the timber against moisture, moulds, mildew and fungal growth. If your windows are small, consider extra ventilation such as an exhaust fan to create an air flow in the room.
- Panelling: try to make sure you select panelling complete with its finish. This will give you a much better feel for how the panelling will look in your 'wet' area as it will always have to be finished to protect against moisture. Remember the 'basic rules' on how dark and light colours affect the spatial feel of your room.
- Profiles: it is a good idea to choose a panelling profile that won't collect too much dust or moisture. Horizontal profiles are great dust collectors and will require extra cleaning time.
- Timber selection: adverse effects on timber panelling can be minimised by the thoughtful selection of timber species. Generally, home owners are guided towards species considered as 'durable' or 'moderately durable', or of relative high density or pressure preservative treated with fungicides. Some of the timbers available and their colours are listed in the following table.

Colour	Species
Cream	blackbutt, celery-top pine, preservative treated radiata, slash pine or hoop pine
Cream-brown	cypress pine
Brown-red	Chilean alerce, brush box, Philippine cedar, jarrah, teak, Californian redwood, spotted gum, turpentine, western red cedar
Grey-brown	tallowwood

- Finishing: most people who put timber panelling in 'wet' rooms do so with the intention of clear finishing, usually over the natural timber colour. In this case it's a good idea to used pre-finished timber where the finish has been applied all round — to the face, the edges, cut ends and back. If you're a do-it-yourselfer and are using raw timber, apply the finish before fixing the panelling to the wall — and make sure to get expert advice and follow the product instructions.

Dos and don'ts of timber panelling for 'wet' rooms

- DON'T use timber panelling in a shower recess or where it would receive frequent wetting.
- DON'T fit timber panelling onto the rim of a bath, basin or tub. Use another material to separate the panelling from the wet area if even by a few centimetres.
- DON'T allow humid or steamy air from wet rooms to fill the wall cavity behind the panelling and so damage the adjacent walls. Fit a vapour barrier behind the panelling if required.
- DO use seasoned panelling and still allow time for panelling to condition in the area in which it will be fixed.
- DO make sure the backs of panels are sealed before fixing in place.
- DO avoid split panels — drill the nail holes to avoid splitting.

Furniture

The tone of any room is really set by the furniture. More than the colours, fittings or design of a home, furniture gives you an instant feeling for the people who live there and their lifestyle. The way you furnish will also determine how guests will feel — whether they'll be relaxed or tense, careful or careless.

Most tastes and budgets are well catered for by the plethora of furniture shops in every city and town — it's not difficult to meet your basic furniture needs. Most furniture is mass produced and comes in readily identifiable styles e.g. country, everyday, designer Italian, reproduction etc.

Some furniture stores can make custom-built furniture to order or you can commission a cabinet-maker or fine craftsperson to do special pieces, either of your design or theirs. And of course, do-it-yourselfers can always make their own — and there is definitely something special about your own handmade furniture taking pride of place in your home.

Furniture might be with you for a long time and it can become part of the family. A cherished kitchen or dining table made from scarce huon pine or Australian cedar may be treasured for generations.

Some people collect antiques with such long-term use in mind. As well as having a beautiful piece of furniture to enjoy it presents, in most cases, a long-term investment. And antiques don't necessarily have to be fancy or expensive. The old chests of drawers that people made from packing cases during the depression of the 1930s would never have been considered precious by their original owners. Made with a timber frame into which slid the packing case drawers, which were sometimes covered with colourful fabric to disguise their plain origins, these old drawers are still around and are much sought after by collectors today.

Your choice of furniture is really only limited by your imagination and your budget, but a lack of funds need not mean you can't have what you want. You might need to be patient — rather than buying a compromise piece it could be better to put up with cheaper furniture and save up for your heart's desire. Most good quality furniture will last a lifetime and is worth waiting for.

It's also possible, if you're prepared to do some research and/or legwork, to obtain precious or good quality pieces quite cheaply through trade magazines, local papers, garage sales, op shops and especially at auctions.

Auctions, however, can be a trap for the unwary — it's easy to get caught up in the atmosphere and buy more than you should. It's probably a good idea to go to a few just to observe before you actually buy anything, to get an idea of what's going on, what things are worth and what the potential pitfalls are. In general, you'll pay less at an auction house than at an on-site deceased estate auction, but if you know what you're doing you can definitely come away with a bargain. Just make sure you factor in the auctioneer's 10–12 per cent on top, and the cost of carrying the furniture.

Antiques ➢ Australian cedar ➢ beds ➢ blackwood ➢ bookcases ➢ buffets ➢ cabinets ➢ cane ➢ chairs ➢ chests ➢ chipboard and hardboard ➢ chrome ➢ couches ➢ desks ➢ dining room tables ➢ dining room chairs ➢ distressed paints ➢ drawers ➢ dressers ➢ dressing tables ➢ French polish ➢ Japanese lacquer ➢ kitchen chairs ➢ kitchen tables ➢ lacquered furniture ➢ leather ➢ marine ply ➢ occasional tables ➢ polyurethane finishes ➢ red gum ➢ silver ash ➢ sofas and armchairs ➢ sideboards ➢ walnut ➢ melamine ➢ paint ➢ plywood ➢ renovating timber furniture ➢ rustic timber finishes ➢ steel ➢ timber finishes ➢ upholstery ➢ vibrant colours ➢ wicker ➢ wood waxes ➢ wrought iron

Antiques

What a definitive and special 'look' antique furniture can give to a room or an entire home — it's extraordinary the style a few antique pieces can bring, and they're usually a good investment too.

Antique furniture often conjours up images of grandma's brittle old chairs which were never allowed to be sat on, or tables that can't take spills and normal wear and tear. But it doesn't have to be like that any more; antique furniture can be functional as well. All furniture wears over time and this is part of its charm — it can also be repaired and restored to its former glory and, with a little time spent over the best type of finish, antique furniture can be versatile and user friendly enough to fit in with today's busiest lifestyle.

Antique furniture has a very blurry time line simply because 'old' and 'antique' mean different things to different people, often depending on their age. Definitively speaking, an antique is something that is more than 100 years old, but to most people an antique can mean something from even the previous generation — furniture from the 1950s and 1960s is often regarded as antique — and that's the way we'll treat it here.

Traditionally in Australia, most of our antiques came from England, just as most of our early immigration did. But now, with our increasingly diverse culture, more and more antiques are coming from different places around the world. Likewise, early Australian antiques were very influenced by English furniture designs, but our fine furniture makers of today, whose work will become the antiques of our grandchildren, have a much broader approach to their work, taking influences from all over the world.

Today, we are free to take whatever antique styles and periods we want and use them to our advantage. We can create art deco, Regency or Federation styles for our home, we can take one period piece only and make it a feature in a modern room, or we can mix and match, using combinations as we want. There are antiques magazines and periodicals, and of course there are antique shops and dealers everywhere. Go and take a look and get some ideas — even if you can't afford antiques you might get some inspiration from which you can create a great decorative theme in your home.

Antique styles and periods

In the Australian context, antique furniture generally breaks down into styles governed by periods in English history followed by the more modern periods in Australian history.

Jacobean: Starting with the reign of James I in 1603 and continuing through three main influences — Renaissance, European and Dutch — until the end of Queen Anne's reign in 1714. Designs were quite 'chunky' in style, especially in the early part of the period, with a lot of intricate carving and inlays. The main timbers used were oak, fruitwoods and walnut, then towards the end of the period lacquers began to be used.

Georgian: Beginning with the reign of George I in 1714 through to the early settlement of Sydney in 1788 and Hobart in 1804 — the early colonial period. Designs were generally less bulky, more refined and sometimes featured the classical motifs of Rome and Greece, called neo-classicism. Timbers used were walnut and mahogany and, as trade increased with the voyages of the European explorers, timbers such as West Indian mahogany were used. The new settlers to Australia were influenced, as you would expect, by styles from their homeland, but they quickly began to use the local timbers such as cedar and casuarina, which grew around Sydney, and blackwood and Huon pine, two of the stunning native timbers of Tasmania.

Regency: The Regency period, named after the Prince Regent who later became George IV, covered more or less the first third of the nineteenth century up until the reign of Queen Victoria in 1837. By this time Australia was becoming well settled with the founding of Brisbane, Perth, Melbourne and Adelaide. Cedar continued its dominance of Australian furniture and was joined by Queensland timbers such as ash and maple and Victorian and New South Wales hardwoods such as red gum, while in Europe oak, mahogany, beech, elm and ash were commonly used. Design in England featured a true classical revival — motifs from the Greek, Egyptian, Assyrian and Roman societies. Australian furniture of this period is called 'colonial' and it tended to follow the 'classical' styles popular in England. However, there was also a lot of plainer, more 'primitive' furniture made that started to show the beginnings of an Australian style.

Victorian: Starting in 1837 and ending in 1901, which coincided with Australian Federation, the Victorian period is a period of repeats and 'revivals'. There was a gothic revival, the rococo revival and the renaissance revival; and intermingled with these were bentwood, Anglo-Japanese and art nouveau styles. In Australia, this late colonial period was a time of rapid population growth and most of the furniture was mass produced, imported from England. There were, however, many fine Australian craftspeople and joiners who produced furniture locally out of the much-loved cedar, Huon pine, blackwood, kauri pine and various hardwoods.

Edwardian: The Edwardian period was a very short period of about a decade at the beginning of the twentieth century dominated by the art nouveau movement — a highly decorative style of sweeping swirls and naturalistic motifs whose most well known proponent is probably Toulouse Lautrec, the French painter. Art nouveau symbolised those seemingly frantic yet romantic years prior to World War I that saw the invention of the aeroplane and motor car and the widespread use of electricity, radio and the telephone. Cedar, kauri pine, maple, silky oaks and various other hardwoods were the popular Australian furniture timbers of the time.

Modern: The rest of the twentieth century featured two main design styles known as 'art deco' and 'the fifties'. In art deco, the intricate decorations of previous periods were replaced with clean, simple lines that, in

themselves, formed the major decoration of the piece. Chair legs became straight and were not turned as they were in previous periods; a table might have some refectory influences but be less chunky. Bakelite, glass and other materials started replacing timber. The industrial twentieth century was starting to have a strong influence over style.

After World War II, when industry and peoples' lives got going again, a new design style spread across the world. It was a mixture of organic shapes and functionality and it really took off from where art deco had stopped prior to the outbreak of the war. Here again, new materials offered extraordinary freedom in design and style, the old world was cast off and we were entering the age of plastic and vinyl, glass, plywood and chrome. Proof of the fact that we are living in an increasingly fast world, 1950s revivals have already taken place at least once and continue to do so.

Antique and timber finishes

Keeping the finish of a special piece of furniture in good order is not difficult; it is when the piece or the finish has been damaged that problems start. If you are good with your hands and an experienced do-it-yourselfer, repairing and restoring furniture can be a pleasurable experience. But if you're not confident, it's always best to seek professional advice.

With any piece of furniture, whether it's antique or modern, it's good to understand something about the materials it is made of and the type of finish — this is especially so when buying and selling antiques because maintaining the original finish should make the piece more valuable.

The four main finishes of antique timber furniture are lacquer, shellac, varnish and wax. As lacquer and varnish weren't used until the late nineteenth century, furniture made before that time is likely to be finished in shellac, wax or both.

Wax

Prior to the technique of French polishing using shellac, beeswax was the most common furniture finish. It has been used for centuries for preserving timber beautifully.

It is applied to the bare timber, giving a warm, satin glow and enhancing the grain. The polish is made from natural beeswax dissolved in gum turpentine, often with some additions such as Brazilian palm wax and sometimes Carnauba wax to make the finish harder. Sometimes oxide powders are added to bring out the colour in a piece of furniture — black, India red, yellow, burnt sienna. But beware! A tiny bit of oxide goes a long way, so use it very sparingly.

Beeswax can be purchased direct from a beekeeper — the natural impurities don't matter — or there are several proprietary brands available from hardware stores and specialist furniture restorers. Be careful when buying prepared wax that the label specifies beeswax and is not a silicone copy — the results won't be the same. Another point to take into consideration with bare timber is that a wax finish will soak into the wood and is very difficult to replace with another finish such as shellac, lacquer or varnish. However, beeswax polish has become very popular again and looks great, especially on pine.

If you haven't tried polishing with wax before, there's no reason why you shouldn't start. But practise on another piece of timber first and make sure you get some expert advice on how to go about it.

Shellac

Shellac and the technique of French polishing began around the 1820s and has really been the number one quality furniture finish since that time. Shellac is derived from 'lac', a resinous secretion from a South-East Asian insect called *Laccifer lacca* (see page 42). The polish is made from shellac crystals dissolved in methylated spirits and normally applied in one of two ways, with a brush or using a soft pad (the French polish method). It is available from good hardware stores either in its crystal form or prepared ready for use.

Shellac seals the timber and provides a beautiful patina that can be waxed over for extra hardness. Alternatively, it can be French polished to a natural lustre. The only problem with French polish is that liquids leave a white stain and hot things mark it too, so it's not the best solution for a tabletop and surfaces that get a lot of day-to-day use. Antique tabletops and worktops are better varnished, another genuine antique finish; this offers them better protection against spills (although not complete protection) while retaining an 'antique' appearance.

Lacquer

Lacquer was developed in Asia to overcome the many problems with shellac — the easy marking and the milky white stain caused by water. It is essentially shellac with some additives and solved most of the problems, but still went a milky white colour with water.

The techniques for the famous Japanese lacquerware were said to have been first introduced into Japan from China. Fine pieces of lacquerware have been found dating back to the seventh century. Some of the traditionally made lacquer work was the result of over 100 coats of lacquer. Lacquerware in Japan was meant for everyday use and has been used for everything from furniture to soup bowls and chopsticks.

Because of its fast drying qualities, lacquer was used on a lot of mass-produced furniture from the late nineteenth century.

Varnish

Varnish is a traditional, oil-based finish that is sometimes 'stained' to a desired colour. These days you can either use traditional varnish or the more modern polyurethanes. However, for an antique a traditional varnish is advisable.

Varnish is applied using a brush. For tabletops and other surfaces it is best to work across the grain first, finishing with the grain. Varnish has the advantage, unlike shellac and lacquer, of drying slowly, so missed bits and 'runs' can be touched up as you go along or even as a final check before you clean up. Varnish may need two coats to achieve a satisfactory finish and can be finished with a coating of beeswax applied with extremely fine steel wool.

Identifying an original finish

Identifying an original finish is a matter of 'practice makes perfect'. Even when you become proficient, there are people out there who may try to hoodwink you, so if you are in any doubt have the piece of furniture checked out by an expert.

- Get to know your antique finishes through regular visits to dealers and by asking questions.
- Look for sanding, wire brush and steel wool marks. Sanding can also lead to rounded edges.
- Take a look underneath the piece — often a new finish will reveal itself with drips and other careless signs.
- A piece that is refinished generally looks in better condition without scratches or chips, those little things that always happen to a piece of furniture over time.
- Look for an old finish underneath the new one.

Here are some ways to help test for an antique finish. But be careful — always choose a concealed part of the furniture and, if you're unsure, have an expert do it for you.

Identifying wax

Wax can be identified in two basic ways. One is to observe the finish. Wax has a subtle but definite patina to it — soft, semi-gloss and honeyed — and it tends to have built up over time, especially in nooks and crannies. So one of the best tests is to simply scrape a tiny out-of-the-way section with your fingernail or pocketknife and see if you get a waxy deposit. Another way is to wrap your finger in a piece of cloth, dip it in some pure gum turpentine and rub a small concealed spot on the furniture. If it 'melts', it's most likely wax. A bit more rubbing should buff it back to its former glory.

Identifying shellac / French polish

The best test for shellac is methylated spirits. Wrap your finger in a small piece of rag, wet in the white spirit and rub a small concealed section of the finish. If it's shellac the finish will dissolve and smooth out as it's rubbed. Then, as the white spirit evaporates it should harden back to its original look — maybe even better.

Identifying lacquer

Lacquer is dissolved by lacquer thinner and paint stripper — but paint stripper removes just about anything so it's not the best test. Wet a small 'finger' of rag with some lacquer thinner and rub a small concealed section of the finish. If it's lacquer the surface will begin to dissolve and smooth out. Within a minute or two the thinner will evaporate and the lacquer harden, leaving a new, shiny surface.

Identifying varnish

Varnish can give the appearance of a slightly filmy finish — sometimes you can lift a corner and peel it back. It has a fairly high oil content so it is not brittle like lacquer and shellac. Basically varnish is not dissovable, but can be removed with paint stripper which makes it blister and crinkle.

French polishing

Dating back to about the 1820s, French polishing was regarded as the ultimate timber finish for the best part of a century. Even now many still regard it that way. Basically, the technique uses shellac dissolved in methylated spirits to create a deep penetrating lustre to timber, the polish soaking deep down into the wood.

French polishing is an involved process that requires practice and persistance. But it also gives a great sense of achievement to have actually done it, because you will have then mastered a wonderful traditional craft and given the most beautiful finish to your piece of furniture.

The polish is rubbed onto the timber finish in a series of 'coats' using a special 'rubber' usually made of a large wad of cotton wool wrapped in linen cloth. First, it is applied in a concentrated form over several stages using various rubbing techniques — with the grain, across the grain, circular motion and figure eight motion. Linseed oil is used to lubricate the polishing if it becomes too dry, light sanding sometimes occurs after the first stage, and the final application is normally a 50/50 dilution with methylated spirits. After all that, there is a final stage called 'spiriting off' using 100 per cent methylated spirits to give the surface a hard, high gloss and to remove any traces of the linseed oil.

Between stages the polish must be allowed to dry and harden, which means the process can take over several days. To finish, you can choose between a deep, shiny natural lustre or, by waxing, a flatter look. Waxing also adds a protective seal, making the polish less susceptible to stains from liquids — wine and other alcoholic drinks dissolve French polish.

French polishing needs regular care and maintenance, depending on how much use the particular piece gets. It is the Rolls Royce of finishes. If you want to give it a go, check out some books at your local library or bookstore and have a chat to your local antique dealer to get some expert advice.

Bedroom furniture

Up until twenty or thirty years ago, bedrooms contained much more furniture than they normally do today. Once there were wardrobes whereas now built-ins, to a large extent, have replaced wardrobes, the large chests of drawers and the dressing tables of yesteryear. Bedrooms today can be quite minimalist — simply a bed, bedside tables and maybe a chair. As well, we are now in the era of the ensuite bathroom, something that only existed in the wealthiest homes thirty years ago.

Bedrooms, like any other room of the house, should reflect your needs and lifestyle. You might be the casual type, or love formality; you may be a compulsive bedtime reader or a person who likes to lie in on the weekends. You may prefer a country feel or prefer it minimalist, even futuristic. Think about your nocturnal lifestyle and work out what's best for you.

Beds

How beds have changed over the centuries! Once an animal skin on a dirt floor, now beds have posturepedic mattresses, crisp bed linen, dreamy feather doonas and all manner of comforts and trappings. One of the most striking comparisons is the huge, ornately carved Jacobean four-poster bed and today's simple bed base and mattress.

Beds are usually constructed of timber, or iron and brass and sometimes can be made of steel, chrome tubing and wrought iron, wood veneer and many other materials as well. Modern mattress bases are constructed around a wooden frame with heavy duty spring wire in the base.

Beds can come in almost any style too, such as the French-style sleigh bed,

To extend the life of a mattress it needs to be turned over and rotated to prevent the mattress forming 'body impressions'.

a range of reproduction styles, quilted bedheads and any number of plain modern bedheads.

Timber beds in solid wood and veneers are mostly finished in varnishes and polishes that show off the natural beauty of the wood; but paint, especially crackling, scrumbling and washes can also look great.

The brass bed was first introduced in the 1820s and became so popular it all but took over from timber right through until the early twentieth century. Brass beds can look wonderful when restored to their former beauty — the rich matt-black iron punctuated with brass 'joints'. Some more up-market varieties are made almost completely of brass.

Whatever your choice, this is one piece of furniture where functionality is important. Everyone knows what it is like when they don't get a good night's sleep.

Mattresses

Modern mattresses are made with coil springs that respond by supporting the body weight of the person sleeping. A good mattress is usually constructed of a quilted fabric cover over a thick layer of foam, then cotton padding followed by more layers of foam over the top of spring wires.

Bedside tables

It's important that bedside tables suit the room, and it's equally important they are functional as well. There's nothing worse than a rickety bedside table — and there are plenty about — where your morning cuppa spills over and your lamp tumbles off just when you least expect it. It's important they are the correct height as well — too low or too high make them difficult to use.

It's a good idea to spend some time thinking about your bedroom lifestyle, just as you would for any other room in the house. For example, if you are an avid bedtime reader it's probably a good idea to have a bedside table that can accommodate all your reading material because, as any reader-holic will admit, piles of books and magazines end up all over the floor.

In a minimalist bedroom where inbuilt cupboards store all your clothes, bedside tables need only complement the bed; and, of course, they are often sold as part of a suite. But when there are other features, such as a beautiful cedar chest of drawers, it's important to consider the colour of other timber in the room or a theme such as wrought iron or caneware.

Chests of drawers and dressing tables

Since the inception of built-in wardrobes, chests of drawers and dressing tables have tended to be in less demand, although many bedroom suites still feature drawers.

Another modern alternative is a storage unit that can store all sorts of things from clothes to a television and video, and these can be constructed out of any number of the modern materials.

A popular antique chest of drawers are those made of Australian red cedar from the late nineteenth and early twentieth centuries. They usually consist of two, three or four broad, deep drawers with an arrangement at the top of two deep 'hat' drawers either side of two shallow 'collar' and trinket draws in the middle. More recently, interesting antique chests from Asia have become available. Otherwise, chests of drawers, often called lowboys these days, are included in bedroom suites and there is a readily available plethora of pine furniture available in stores that proliferate in our cities and country towns.

Bookcases

For the bookworms amongst us, there are never enough bookcases in the home and books end up being poked into the shelves sideways and stacked on the shelves. There's a lesson to be learned here: when bookworms are working out the number of bookshelves needed in the home, they should double it.

Bookshelves do two things: they store books and they take care of books, so if you have very precious books and you live in a difficult climate it's worth considering shelves with ultraviolet glass-fronted doors to protect the books against dust, humidity and bright daylight, all of which can fade covers badly over time.

Large furniture stores and pine furniture manufacturers have made an excellent range of affordable bookshelves available. There is a large assortment of different sizes in all sorts of different finishes, and many of them have add-ons so that you can easily go higher and wider if you need more storage space. As well, it's handy if the shelves can be adjusted for bigger and smaller books.

Bookshelves follow a pretty universal design, so it's really the size and finish where you get the real differences. Take the time to think about the best bookshelf layout for your room. You may have so many books that you have to cover the four walls, floor to ceiling, with shelves. If so you're going to get that warm, cosy library look. On the other hand your book collection may be much more contained, in which case there are lots of design possibilities open to you. For instance, your room may suit a set of low shelves running along a wall. This can be great because you can use the top for ornaments, knick-knacks, photos and vases of flowers. You can stagger the height too so that the shelves 'step' up and down— there's no need be a slave to rigid design.

Finishes are normally a range of timber veneers and paint. Timber veneers tend to fall into three main groups: light colours such as beech and ash, mid-colours such as maple and creamy oak, and dark colours such as cedar and teak. This is where the decision-making comes in — in making sure you get the right colour for your room. Light colours will look more airy and spacious; dark colours will give it more warmth and cosiness.

The other popular finish — paint — offers a marvellous range of choices because of the myriad of different colours and styles available — from brightly coloured gloss to subdued satin colours, from crackle glazes to washes. The 'rubbed on' antique look can look great too. Don't be afraid to experiment, but do get some expert advice first on what measures you can take if you end up with something you don't like.

Most bookshelves these days are made of pine or veneered particleboard, but if you want to go that one step further there is always the option of solid timber. For the do-it-yourselfer bookshelves are not that hard to build, so you could end up with custom-made bookshelves in the timber of your choice.

There is one further bookshelf and that's the bookshelf with doors, or the book cabinet. There are many modern and antique styles available, some dating back to about the 1700s, after books became affordable and available to everyone. Like other cabinets and cupboards in the home, bookshelves can be either free standing or built into the wall. The style you choose should depend largely on the overall style you have, or are creating, for the room. If you have an Edwardian house, for example, you may wish to style your bookshelves to blend with any original cornices or trimmings.

Cabinets, dressers, sideboards and storage units

Cabinets have always been in great demand for storage in the home. Some may be used to store sports trophies, others wine, while others may store precious crystal and ceramic pieces. Whatever their use, cabinets still enjoy great popularity and come in all sorts of different shapes and sizes.

In Jacobean times, cabinets were often big and solid and made of heavy oak, while in colonial Australia red cedar was a favourite material. Today cabinets can be made of any number of different materials — laminates, timber, stainless steel, plywood and melamine to name but a few.

Dating back to earlier than most people can remember, dressers are cabinets too but tend to be specialised units used in the kitchen. The pine dresser, dating back to the mid 1850s, has made a resurgence in the last twenty or thirty years and today is an extremely popular piece of furniture in the home. With plates stored 'on show' on the shelves, a dresser can give your kitchen a great 'country' feel. Another style of dresser that now is also very sought after is the art deco kitchen dresser from the 1930s. It usually has dimpled glass doors and a comprehensive set of drawers to store cutlery and other kitchen needs.

Sideboards and buffets were designed as serveries — the prepared food would be brought from the kitchen and served at the sideboard. Dating back to the mid 1600s, essentially they are a working height table-top with two or three drawers and cupboards underneath that hold all the crockery and cutlery. They have changed in style as times have changed — many were made of dark oak but now, while not as popular as they once were, they are often made of veneer.

Cane

Cane is a very versatile material; you can make just about anything with it — a whole house if you like — as they have in some tropical regions. Tables, chairs and lounges are the most popular pieces of furniture, but over time many other items have been made of cane — beds, hallstands, cabinets, sideboards, drawers, chests, basinettes and even prams.

In Asian and South-East Asian countries cane has been used for centuries — and first became popular in Europe with trade between the two continents in the nineteenth century. As colonial Australia was influenced by most things English, cane became popular here too at about the same time, although the idea had travelled halfway across the world and back again before it was accepted.

In Asian countries cane has always been a broadly universal furniture and decorative timber, but when it was first introduced in Europe, it was used to furnish verandahs and conservatories. By Edwardian times it was popular for use in the bedroom and children's rooms and for other furniture such as plant stands, tea trolleys, rocking chairs and day beds. It was about this time that the famous verandah lounge made of split cane and seagrass, the lazyboy, first became popular.

The word 'cane' is used for furniture made of a number of different materials — cane, rattan, wicker and seagrass. Cane is the dried stem of the bamboo plant. It is long and hollow and comes in many different thicknesses and lengths. Rattan is the stem of another palm, while wicker is actually the shoot of the willow tree. It is usually thin and very flexible. Seagrass, similar to the floor covering, is a sea plant spun and twisted into useful lengths just like many other fibres.

Naturally the different materials create different looks and styles and they are often used together on the one piece of furniture. As well, the furniture is often constructed using a wooden frame with the cane, rattan, wicker or seagrass acting as the 'superstructure' — willow was always popular in Asia and Europe, whereas other timbers were used in Australia.

Cane furniture is normally varnished and waxed to retain its beautiful rich honeyed colour, although it was often painted as well — usually white. During the late Edwardian and art deco periods of the twentieth century the binding, used to secure different sections of the piece together, was dyed red or green. Decorative approaches of this kind kept the furniture 'informal' in style.

Chairs

As a child I used to draw floor plans of my dream home. I also used to draw pictures of my wedding dress, but that's another story.

Ever since I saw June Bronhill in 'The Sound of Music' in Melbourne when I was only a few years old, I've been fascinated by atmosphere and lighting and the effects that could be created. My family home was middle class late 1950s and 1960s, a mixture of reproduction Queen Anne furniture from Myers and a few more 'modern' things — laminex tables, built-in louvred wardrobes, glass-fronted display cabinet — pretty typical of its era.

When I left home and went to uni I went through or rather began my op shop hippy phase — roadside throw-out furniture draped with Indian bed covers, bean bags, mattresses on the floor and bookcases made with Besser blocks and timber planks.

In my twenties and thirties I travelled a little and rented an assortment of flats or houses, and I discovered pot plants as a decorating item. I also bought very cheaply some wonderful art deco furniture (working girl's flat-type furniture) from a production I was in for Film Australia called 'Weekly's War' set in World War II, about the role the *Women's Weekly* played in keeping up morale during the war. I bought other furniture and pictures from op shops, some of which I still have today — style was not something I thought about then. Functionality and basic needs were the extent of my considerations.

What would we do without chairs; and how many of us have our favourite chair — the one we collapse into after a hard day at the office or at the end of a long day. Just about everyone has their favourite chair.

Up until the nineteenth century most people rested their weary bones on stools or benches; chairs, which first became common a couple of centuries earlier, were really only for the more financially comfortable. Later on, in the nineteenth century, the industrial age meant chairs could be mass produced and therefore became available for everyone.

Two of the early mass-produced chairs were the bentwood chair, developed in the 1840s, and the spindleback or Federation chair, so named because it was produced around the time of Australian Federation and featured nationalistic motifs such as the kangaroo, wildflowers and even the Australian coat of arms. Up until this time chairs had all been handcrafted and followed the styles of other antique periods (see Antique styles and periods, page 112).

With the onset of the twentieth century all sorts of materials became available to the chair maker — tubular steel and chrome followed by plastic — and craftspeople were able to create chairs with looks, strength and resilience that had never been seen before.

Choosing a chair

The chair is one of the most important pieces of household furniture and it's important that it's comfortable, looks great and is long wearing — chairs get the most wear and tear of just about any piece of furniture. The following list gives you just an inkling of the many types of chairs to choose from.

- Jacobean armchair: dating from the 1600s, this large, bulky, quite ornately carved chair was usually made of oak, elm or one of the fruitwoods. As the century proceeded, it became increasingly upholstered and ornate.
- William and Mary armchair: less emphasis on ornately carved wood and more on upholstery on these chairs dating from the late 1600s.
- Chippendale chair: named after cabinetmaker and furniture designer Thomas Chippendale, these chairs date from about 1750 and feature a much more delicate style — Chippendale was influenced by Chinese furniture design and the European Gothic style.

- Georgian dining chair: a classical revival marked the main influence of these chairs dating from the 1830s — fairly plain upholstered seat and back with carved legs, often with an Egyptian lotus motif.
- Australian cottage chairs — also from this period come the first of the chairs of the early colonial period. While taking some of the Georgian influences from England, they were a plain, solid-looking chair.
- Bentwood chair: dating from the 1840s, this could well be awarded the prize for the first mass-produced chair. It was certainly the first of the 'common' or 'cottage' chairs and was constructed of beech and elm that was bent using steam to form the shape of the chair. It had a plaited cane seat inside a round frame.
- Spindleback chairs: the Australian version of these American-designed chairs came into production in the 1870s and was produced by Susman and Kornblum at their factory in Ballarat, Victoria. They were a simple, study chair with, as the name suggests, a set of spindles within a frame forming the back of the chair.
- Federation chair: a spindleback chair dating from 1900 and featuring Australian motifs such as the kangaroo, the waratah and other wildflowers and even the coat of arms, but these are now rare.
- Edwardian cane verandah chair: also dating from 1900, these chairs echoed the more informal style of the Edwardian period with a mix of influences as diverse as Japanese furniture and the art nouveau movement in Europe.
- Dining room carver: all through the twentieth century the 'carver' chair was popular in dining room settings. They had arms and there were usually two, one for each end of the table. Their name came from it being the chair from which the meat was carved.
- Cesca chair: possibly the most famous twentieth century chair, it originated from the Bauhaus School

in Germany and is still popular today. It is constructed of chromed tubular steel and is shaped like an ‘s’. The seat and back are either made of cane held in a frame or leather folded over the steel frame and stitched tight.

- Kitchen and dining room chair: this 1930s mass-produced workhorse of the home became prevalent in this period. Often made of pine, this plain, serviceable piece of furniture was the inspiration for many styles of the following decades. A more refined version, often upholstered and made from blackwood or oak, had more formal applications such as dining room chairs.

Couches, sofas and lounge chairs

The hardest room for me is always the lounge room — how to arrange the seating so that it doesn't end up looking like a doctor's waiting room.

A few years ago I saved up and bought a really comfortable, good quality couch and it's the best investment I ever made and will last a lifetime, and it's incredibly comfortable and comforting. It's as big as a single bed and many guests have chosen to sleep on it by the fire rather than get up and go to the spare room!

Choosing the colour was agonising — for sure I drove the salesman to distraction, but I opted for a deep rusty red. The colour dictates every other choice in the room because the couch is so big and dominant, but I've become much braver over the years, inspired by the increasing use of rainbow colours in fashion and design. There seem to be few rules about colour these days — it really is a case of anything goes — as long as it pleases you.

There have been a lot of inventions in the last millennium — but couches, where you can flop down in front of the telly or curl up in front of the fire with a good book, are one of the great inventions of all time.

Couches, in their original form as the settee, first made their way into homes in the late 1600s. They were quite formal in their design then — like an elongated carver chair — and none too comfortable either. Couches and sofas as we know them today first appeared on the scene in the late 1700s, but it was really not until the 1900s that they became hugely popular, so much so that no modern home today is complete without one.

The lounge, sofa or couch, whichever you prefer to call it — the names are almost synonymous these days — has gone through a number of changes, all mirroring their period of history. The early lounge suites usually consisted of about nine bulky pieces constructed mainly of timber with upholstered seats and backs: a chaise longue, a gentleman's chair, a lady's chair and six dining room-style chairs. Often these had a balloon back. It was a very formal arrangement and often not very comfortable.

Comfort first appeared, strangely enough, in those strict and formal Victorian times of the mid to late 1800s. This was the classic 'Chesterfield', a plush and super-comfortable couch almost always made of leather. However, it wasn't until the 1930s with the club or Genoa lounge that comfort, above all else, became the most important feature of this wonderful piece of furniture.

With the marvellous range available to us these days through modern designs, antique reproductions and antiques themselves, you can find a couch to suit any home, big or small. Lounges are fairly bulky items and can take up a lot of room in a confined space, so it's a good idea to think about the size and bulk when you're choosing your preferred couch. And, of course, for a small apartment, you can always have a sofa bed for those spontaneous or unexpected guests.

Choosing couches and lounge chairs

Here are a few of the styles available.

- **Settee:** the forerunner of the modern lounge, the settee was really a carver chair widened to accommodate more than one person — usually it was a two-seater. Settees are usually made of a wooden frame with a slatted back and cabriole legs. The arm (often winged) and back are upholstered, with the seat consisting of fitted cushions. Today, small sofas and couches are often called settees, but strictly speaking they are not.

- **Chaise longue:** the chaise longue looks like a cross between a lounge and a day bed and is more of a reclining lounge than the ones we're familiar with today. It is made of a wooded frame and heavily padded seat with a padded 'rest' at one end, the back consisting of a wooden frame, padded on top, but usually only continuing for about 7/8 the length of the couch. The name 'chaise longue' comes from the French meaning 'long seat'.
- **Wing-back armchairs:** these date from about the early to mid 1700s and have changed very little in two and a half centuries. Winged-back armchairs were built with comfort in mind; such comfort in fact, that the wings were designed to shelter the incumbent from drafts. Often built on a mahogany frame, they were padded and sprung throughout and upholstered in various luxurious coverings such as leather, velvet, tapestry and chintz, making them ideal for bedrooms and drawing rooms alike.
- **Miner's couch:** colonial Australia's contribution to the evolvement of the lounge, these interesting couches were usually made from red cedar, pine or blackwood and were easily dismountable for the 'miner on the move'. The wood-framed design included a slatted base, large backboard made of solid timber and scrolled arms joined by a number of spindles.
- **Club (Genoa) lounge:** dating from the art deco period of the 1920s and 1930s, the club lounge suite was the first of the modern lounge suites as we know them today. With a few exceptions very little has changed in design and concept since then, the main difference being the materials used for construction. Each suite consisted of a three-seater lounge and two super-comfortable armchairs; and everything was padded for comfort — the back, the seat and the arms.

Design influences

Furniture is a real definer of a room's style. If you start with a bare room, its personality changes depending on what sort of furniture you put in it. You can cram lots of furniture in and make it look warm, cosy and cluttered; or you can have the bare minimum and make it look cool, open and spacious. The Japanese are masters at this — one of the secrets to good design is simplicity.

I remember as a child my parents bought a lounge/dining suite of matching reproduction Queen Anne style furniture and our lounge looked exactly like a showroom.

The beauty of decorating now is that styles are personal and eclectic is fine. Nobody minds if colonial mixes with Balinese, or stark minimalist is augmented by Victorian.

Juxtaposition of pieces, whether furniture or ornaments, is really a question of what you like and where you like it. Play with furniture — you can always put it back the way it was before if you're not happy with the results.

If you're redecorating a room, or starting out from scratch, there's centuries and hundreds of cultures worth of ideas out there just waiting to be used. Some are right under your nose, so to speak, on the time frame of things. In the art deco period of the 1930s and the 'modern' period of the 1950s and 1960s, furniture went through a revolution of change, partly due to the fantastic range of new materials that were invented in the first half of the twentieth century, and partly due to the designers who burst onto the scene in Europe and America following the great European art movements of the early 1900s. The world was really changing and it seemed appropriate that the way people lived did too.

Prior to the 1920s just about every piece of furniture imaginable was made of timber. But then came steel and fabricated steel and suddenly we had chrome-plated tubular steel; and the designers at the famous German institution called the Bauhaus put that to good use and suddenly we had those wonderful cantilevered tubular steel chairs that stayed popular for over 60 years and are still in demand today. So art, culture and technology worked hand in hand.

Plywood was invented, and this meant wood could be bent and shaped like never before. Plywood could be made as wide as you wanted — usually between four and eight times the width of solid milled timber. In the 1920s another substance, bakelite, a by-product of petroleum and the forerunner of plastic, began to be used for radio sets, place mats and even table tops. It was heat and stain resistant. In the 1950s the invention of plastic meant that raw materials for furniture were now malleable and could be cast into any shape the furniture maker wanted. And we had what became known as the womb chair, the plastic moulded chair and the stacking chair. Now anything was possible.

But we are not only dependent on recent history for our inspiration; we can look right back in time through the various antique periods. The medieval refectory look, a major influence on the modern country look, is still popular as is, for many Australians, the furniture of our own colonial period — beautiful pieces made of cedar and Huon pine — which are now very valuable and are regarded with great affection.

Even more exciting are the cultural influences open to us today. Australia's multicultural mix means a home is likely to have influences from any one of 50 or more different cultures. Apart from old England, Scandinavia and Italy have both been big influences on furniture design; and our increasing awareness of our near neighbours offers us some great furniture solutions. Bali has been a big influence, especially in the warm temperate and tropical regions; Japanese design has influenced us too and we needn't stop there.

So there's a lot to be discovered in the history books on art, design and architecture and by simply visiting our neighbours. They can give you a thousand new inspirations!

Veneer

The art of applying and finishing veneers has been developed over many centuries and dates back as far as the ancient Egyptians. Veneers provide an attractive and practical alternative to solid timber, as they can be used in many building and decorating situations such as walls and ceilings, cupboards, shelves, doors and furniture. More importantly, as veneers are cheaper than solid timber the look of expensive and rare timbers can be obtained at a fraction of the cost.

Wood veneer is the most economical way of maximising the use of precious wood resources. About 40 sheets of veneer can be taken from wood only 25 mm thick.

Veneer is produced by slicing or peeling timber logs to approxiamately 0.6 mm. The grain or pattern in the wood can be joined and matched in a number of ways but the most common is like a book. The veneer is folded out like the centre of a book, where one veneer leaf is the mirror

image of the facing leaf. It is possible to create a range of design effects by matching and repeating patterns.

Veneer is usually adhered to a solid base that might be:

- Particleboard (chipboard), a strong, stable and inexpensive base made from small chips of wood bonded together with glue under pressure.
- MDF or medium density fibreboard, which is used when the edges of the base board are going to be exposed. MDF is made from fibres of wood bonded together with resin under pressure.
- Plywood, which is made up of layers of veneer bonded together. Usually two or more plies are bonded together, with the grain going in alternate directions for added strength.
- Solid wood, which is used mainly where strength is important such as doors.

The final appearance and performance of wood veneer furniture will greatly depend on the finishing process. Before you begin the surface must be smooth, clean and dry. Heavy sanding is not recommended, as this will break through the wood surface. The wide range of finishing products on the market that are suitable for conventional timber surfaces are also suitable for veneer surfaces. These include stains, sealers and clear polyurethane finishes, which bring out the beauty of the wood and, at the same time, preserve and protect the surface from moisture and wear and tear. It is important to select the right finish for veneer furniture — for example, a bed would not need the same durable coating as a kitchen sideboard or cabinet. For bathrooms and kitchens, polyurethane has excellent water resistance and scuff and mark resistance, whereas for bedroom furniture a simple to use and fast drying nitrocellulose finish will suffice.

Follow the manufacturer's directions closely and the results will be worth the effort.

Furniture timbers

Nature really excelled when it created trees. Not only do they live for a very long time in their natural state as forests and woodlands, wood lives on for another lifetime as furniture. What a beautiful substance timber is: beautiful to touch and, with its elegant grain and patina, beautiful to look at too; and when it is crafted into a superb piece of furniture it makes you feel that all the forces of nature have come together to create a piece of beauty.

Furniture timbers fall into two categories: softwoods and hardwoods. The softwoods are the pines and conifers and the cedars. The hardwoods are the oaks, gum trees, blackwood, ash, teak, mahogany and the maples, to name a few. Softwoods, as the name suggests, are often lighter and easier to work with, but hardwoods have many advantages as well, one being that they don't suffer from knocks and scrapes as easily.

Here is a list of the timbers and their qualities commonly used in furniture-making.

Australian timbers

Ash

Mountain ash and alpine ash are members of the eucalypt family and are also known as Tasmanian oak because of the grain's resemblance to English oak. Ash species vary in colour from the more common greyish white to a darker yellowish brown and have a straight grain.

A hardwood, this timber has been used mainly since the early 1900s — except when the early pioneers in the mountain regions of Victoria and New South Wales used it to fashion their primitive furniture. It planes and bends well and was often used for bentwood chairs.

Blackwood

Also known as Tasmanian blackwood, where it is most prolific, this hardwood grows in the cooler, wetter regions of the eastern states of Australia. It has a beautiful dark, golden syrup colour with a straight (sometimes wavy) grain and, when polished, it takes on a beautiful patina. For cabinetmakers it has the additional advantages of being lightweight and strong, which has made it an extremely popular timber for chairs, dining room tables, dressers and sideboards. This is one of Australia's truly classical furniture timbers.

Cedar

There are two very romantic Australian timbers, cedar and Huon pine. Sadly, both timbers are now very rare, cut to near extinction because of their popularity and qualities as beautiful furniture timbers.

Cedar is a softwood with a straight, open grain that

has a beautifully sweet, spicy scent when sawn. It grew in the coastal forests of New South Wales, with the mature timber being a beautiful rich red. Colour variance occurred in trees that were cut young or grew in cooler regions. With the latter, trees from southern New South Wales had a tighter grain and were harder and lighter in colour.

Perhaps because of its similar appearance to mahogany, cedar was prized by joiners and cabinetmakers in colonial Australia where it was considered the ideal furniture timber. It finished beautifully into a warm, brooding red, especially when polished with shellac and wax, and it was very easily worked. Tables, chairs, bedroom chests of drawers, buffets and bookcases are all pieces in which cedar works beautifully.

Huon pine

Huon pine is native to Tasmania and one of Australia's most beautiful furniture timbers. It is a golden honey-coloured softwood with a straight, tight grain and a wonderful silky patina.

The trees are very slow growing and it takes at least 500 years for the trunks to grow to half a metre in diameter. It also contains a special oil, methyl eugenol, that repels insects and, together with the tight structure of the wood, makes it very long lasting. In nineteenth century Tasmania it was often used for boat building, but by the 1880s had become scarce and is rarely available these days as timber.

With its fine grain and silky patina Huon pine makes wonderful golden-coloured furniture, including dining tables, dressers, sideboards and bedroom furniture.

Jarrah

Found exclusively in Western Australia, jarrah is a member of the eucalyptus family. It is often referred to as Australian mahogany because it usually darkens with age to resemble its European namesake. Jarrah is a heavy, rich, red-brown even-grained hardwood and was often used for furniture that needed extra sturdiness — library shelving, offices and large dining room settings — though there are many examples where it has been used for smaller domestic furniture as well.

Other pines

The other Australian pines used to make furniture are hoop pine (also known as Richmond River pine) and kauri pine. There are two species of kauri, one from Queensland and the other from New Zealand. All three softwoods were used extensively from the mid nineteenth century until about the 1930s to make cheaper, mass-produced furniture such as kitchen dressers, some of which have become valuable antiques today.

The timbers vary in colour from cream through pale yellow to gold with straight fine grains. The timber tends to darken over time and has an attractive golden colour when finished with shellac and wax.

Queensland maple

Queensland maple is a hardwood that was used extensively in Victorian times for beds, wardrobes, dressing tables and pianos. It was also used as a veneer, its straight, sometimes curly grain imitating walnut and mahogany when stained.

A hard yellow-white to tan timber that finishes very well, Queensland maple is regarded as an exceptionally fine wood for all types of cabinetmaking.

Red box and river red gum

These famous trees, which grow on the vast inland flood plains and beside rivers, are real icons of rural Australia. Timber doesn't come much harder or heavier than red gum and red box and for that reason they have been used consistently for fencing, rough-hewn sheds and sometimes flooring. However, more recently, as craftspeople have continued their search for a very Australian look, these timbers have been used more and more — often for flooring, but also for kitchen benches, big bold dining tables and sometimes sideboards.

Silky oak

With its highly 'decorative' and complex grain, silky oak is the most distinctive of Australian furniture timbers. It grows mainly in Queensland but can be found in other mainland states as well. It can vary in colour from reddish through tan back to quite golden colours and was often stained in the old days to resemble English oak.

With its distinctive grain it is an excellent furniture timber, and is especially attractive on small pieces such as jewellery boxes and inlays.

Exotic timbers

Beech

Beech is a pale creamy white hardwood with a straight, even grain — it is easily worked and light in weight. It has been used for furniture, especially chairs, and for many centuries was the major wood used in bentwood chairs where it was often stained to resemble more expensive timbers such as mahogany.

Camphor-wood

With a colour and grain quite similar to mahogany, this native to South-East Asia is a species of cinnamon tree. Due to its special moth-repelling scent it was used for chests and clothes trunks.

Ebony

Ebony is a very hard, black timber from South-East Asia and West Africa that was more often used for making piano keys, violin fingerboards, drawer and cupboard knobs, and decorative inlays than for complete pieces of furniture.

Elm

With its pale to reddish brown colour and dark, broad grain, elm is quite similar in many respects to oak but was used often in 'country-style' furniture. It is a hardwood — a native of Europe, North America and Asia — and has been a prominent furniture timber since Roman times. It finishes well, especially with a linseed oil polish and wax.

Fruitwoods

Fruitwoods is a group term used for fruit trees such as cherry, apple, plum and pear. These are all hardwoods and are not easy to distinguish from each other, excepting cherrywood.

Mahogany

Mahogany could be called the prince of furniture timbers — ever since it impressed Queen Elizabeth I way back in the late sixteenth century. For a hundred years or so it was used mainly as decorative inlays but then, around 1730, whole pieces started being made of the wood following the demise of the supply of walnut due to wars and severe winters.

It has a beautiful grain with tight texture and great strength and hardness. Its colour too is a magnificent red, similar to Australian cedar. Essentially there are two species of mahogany: West Indian and African, which doesn't have the same tightness in texture. Mahogany is a great timber for all types of furniture — it makes wonderful table tops while at the same time being easily worked for intricate carving on sideboards and other ornate pieces.

Oak

Oak is the great traditional furniture timber of western Europe and especially England, where it has been used ever since furniture was made there. It can be used for any piece of furniture at all — tables, chairs, cupboards, dressers, beds and many more. The English (or European oak) takes about 200 years to grow to maturity and when it's first cut after seasoning for a couple of years, it can have a creamy or pinkish brown colour. As it ages with use and polishing it darkens — hence our association with it as a very dark and sombre wood of medieval England.

One of the features of oak is its imposing grain — when you rub your fingers over it you can almost feel it. It is a strong, tough timber that can be easily worked and bent if needed.

Walnut

Walnut is a native of Europe and North America, where it is called Virginian or black walnut. Of the walnut grown in England and Europe, the French and Italian varieties were the most favoured by furniture makers. Walnut reigned supreme as a furniture timber from about the mid 1600s until about 1730 — some called it 'the age of walnut'.

Walnut is characterised by its warm grey-brown colour and straight grain, although it was also prized for its 'ornate', curly patterns (called 'curls' and 'burrs') in its grain which occur in the roots and at the junction between the trunk and branches ('oyster walnut'). At these sections the timber was usually cut as a veneer for all sorts of superior furniture.

Recycling, renovating and finishing timber furniture

Considering the cost of new furniture, restoring old timber furniture is a rewarding and inexpensive means of redecorating your home — and it can completely change the look of your home as well. There are a huge range of finishes that can be applied to the furniture once the restoration is complete. The key to success is careful surface preparation.

The process of preparing old furniture for a new life can be time consuming, but it can be made easy providing a few basic steps are followed.

Stripping

Stripping is often necessary to remove all of the old paint or finish from a piece of furniture before you can attempt to apply a new fresh finish. The two main methods of stripping are hand stripping with methylated spirits or a proprietary stripper, and stripping in a caustic soda bath.

Hand stripping is most suitable for cedar, walnut, mahogany, veneered wood or any of the fine-grained timbers generally used for antique furniture. The commercial caustic soda method is used for large jobs such as doors, wardrobes and tables because it is quick, effective and comparatively inexpensive. Note that caustic soda can discolour some timbers quite badly — seek advice before embarking on this method to avoid a disappointing outcome.

Sanding

Stripped or unfinished furniture must be sanded as smooth as possible before any new finish is applied. This is also important for the end result will in large part reflect the amount of effort that has been put into a smooth finish. When sanding, it is advisable to wear a simple face mask so the dust particles are not inhaled.

Sanding tips

Patience and elbow grease will pay great dividends in the end.

- Sand with progressively finer grades of sandpaper, starting with medium or fine grades and finishing with very fine. Always rub with the grain to avoid scratches.
- Use a sanding block on flat surfaces to prevent unevenness and rounded edges.
- For curved or irregular surfaces, use strips of sandpaper to get into the difficult crevices and shapes. Pads of medium to fine steel wool can also be used for difficult areas.
- If you use an electric sander, do not use a circular one because it will not sand in a straight line and the circular motion can leave marks on the wood surface that will show up when the new finish is applied. Always sand with the grain.

> Once you are satisfied with the sanded finish, dust down the piece of furniture thoroughly. The best way to do this is with a tack rag, which you can buy at your paint dealer or you can make one from a piece of lint-free cotton cloth. Just dip the cloth into varnish that has been diluted with an equal amount of turpentine or mineral spirits. Wring out the cloth until almost dry.

Tip for staining timber furniture — always test the stain on the back or underneath before you blithely spread it where it can't be changed if you don't like it. Many stains don't look like you expect them to when they're applied, so be careful — it's a pain in the neck to sand it back and start again.

Finishing

There are many different finishes that can be used to restore a piece of furniture to its former glory or, if you prefer, give a new outlook on life with something different from the original finish. For timber there are traditional finishes described earlier in this chapter (see page 116) and there are a huge range of paints and stains available too. The following offers a few hints on that much forgotten craft, staining.

Staining

Stains are used to colour wood and emphasise its grain. They can also be used to make the colour of one type of wood match another or to tint patched areas to match the rest of the piece. Stains should only be used on bare, smooth, clean and dry wood.

Of the many stains on the market, there are two that seem to be the most popular: penetrating resin stains and pigmented oil or wiping stains. The first is a clear resinous coating that sinks deep into the wood, darkening the natural appearance. As penetrating resin stains are also

Hand stripping tips

Hand stripping is usually carried out with a proprietary stripper or methylated spirits, depending on the timber. It's important to get the right advice on the most suitable stripper for the particular timber. With the use of paint strippers, make sure the work area is very well ventilated and avoid breathing in the dangerous vapours. Also, wear gloves and cover any exposed skin.

- Buy a good quality grade of commercial paint or varnish remover. Commercial strippers of different strengths are available from all good hardware stores. Ensure the remover you purchase is suitable for the wood being stripped.
- Pour some remover into a clean can.
- With a paint brush, spread the remover liberally on one small section of the furniture at a time. Stroke in one direction only.
- Leave to soak into the surface or until the finish has softened right through to the wood — usually 5 to 15 minutes.
- Scrape the softened finish with a scraper or dull putty knife. Wipe off the old finish from the scraper onto old newspaper. For carved or grooved surfaces, an old toothbrush or a pointed implement will help to get into crevices. On very old furniture with many coats of paint, several soak and scrape operations may be required.
- Woods such a walnut, oak or mahogany have an open grain that will retain some of the old finish. To remove it, saturate a pad of steel wool with some of the remover and rub the wood, working with the grain. A stiff bristle brush can also be helpful.
- Once the finish has been removed, wipe the wood dry with clean dry cloths. Follow the directions on the remover label. A final wipe with mineral spirits or turpentine is sometimes recommended, since some removers contain wax and this must be removed from the wood surface before it can be resurfaced.

a finish, a coat of wax is all that is necessary once it is dry.

Pigmented oil or wiping stains are more controllable. If the wood becomes too dark it can be lightened with minimum effort by rubbing with turpentine while still wet, or by sanding when dry. Before using an oil stain, clean the surface with a cloth dampened in turpentine or mineral spirits.

Tips for staining furniture

Do less conspicuous areas first, saving the front and top for last. Always wipe in the direction of the grain. End grain wood is more absorbent, so wipe with some linseed oil first to slow down the absorption.

Bleaching and filling

In addition to staining, two other processes may be needed depending on the type of wood. If you want to lighten the original colour of the wood, you may want to bleach it. A bleach can be obtained at almost any paint store. Be sure to follow the manufacturer's directions and wear protective gloves when using it. If you are working on an open pore wood such as walnut, oak or mahogany, use a wood filler to obtain a smooth finish. These fillers are available in different colours and a neutral shade that can be tinted with the stain you have used. Both wood filler and bleaches are applied before staining or finishing.

Clear finishing

Once the piece has been stripped, sanded and stained (if necessary), then finishing is the only remaining process left to do.

Probably *the* most popular finish is clear polyurethane. It is usually available in gloss, semi-gloss or flat depending on the finish you require. All have good water and scuff resistance, although the flat one is somewhat less so. Consider whether the piece of furniture will get a lot of day-to-day use or will be in an area such as a kitchen or bathroom — polyurethane is ideal for these areas. All the polyurethanes are resistant to solvents such as alcohol, turpentine or similar. An important factor to remember, especially with children about, is that these finishes are also non-toxic; but ensure that you check the label first.

With time and patience anyone can make a once tatty, forgotten piece of furniture come back to life again. Who knows — it may become a valuable antique one day!

Tips for applying polyurethane

Read all instructions carefully and follow these steps:

- Some polyurethanes can take a long time to dry, so ensure that the area where you work is dust free and has adequate ventilation.
- Polyurethane is flammable, so take care with naked lights and do not smoke.
- Wipe the surface with turpentine to remove every possible trace of dust before applying the first coat.
- Thin the first coat with turpentine (50 ml per litre), mixing gently. Do not stir, as unwanted air bubbles will appear.

- Apply with a good quality natural bristle brush. Dip the brush into the polyurethane one third the length of the bristles. To remove any excess, tap the bristle tips lightly against the inside of the container.
- Avoid wiping the brush against the rim of the can as this causes tiny air bubbles to form, making it very difficult to obtain a smooth finish.
- Brush on the surface, then work the brush at right angles to the original direction of application.
- 'Tip off' by pulling an almost dry brush along at a 30 degree angle.
- Allow to dry completely.
- Sand lightly with a fine grade paper or steel wool. Dust well and wipe. Repeat this step between each coat (three coats should do).

Tables

Tables were once the sole domain of timber — every table was made of wood — but now, while timber still remains the most popular table material, tables can also be made from a huge range of other materials the modern world has invented including plastics, laminates, steel and glass. Mums and dads will remember the extraordinarily popular laminex table from the 1950s with its legs made from chrome tubular steel.

A big kitchen table is still as friendly and endearing as it always was when the kettle hissed gently on the wood stove and the smell of baking scones wafted from the oven. A big dining table, too, often signals that this home has lots of friends visit for long cheerful meals of scrumptious food and wine. Next to the chair, the table is the home's most cherished possession — we eat our meals at it, we argue over it, we read newspapers on it, school assignments are done on it, dress patterns are cut out on it. What could be more useful?

There are different tables for different purposes and it's a good idea when you're choosing a new table to carefully consider all the things for which it could be used; this will have a lot to do with choosing the best finish. Will it stand alone in the dining room, beautifully polished, never used except for the odd dinner party, or will it be something that lives out every moment of a family's life? Think about colours too — dark or light — and about how it will look against the rest of your decor.

Breakfast tables

In the old days Grandma's family would most likely have had a breakfast table made of cedar, pine or perhaps maple, which would have either been in the kitchen or tucked away in the corner of the living room or closed-in verandah.

Dining tables

Dining tables are designed for formal meals. More often than not dining tables are made of timber and are usually very well finished with varnish, French polish and/or wax, although many these days are finished with polyurethane so that they're easy to look after and resistant to heat and stains. Whereas kitchen tables would usually be made of pine, dining room tables would normally be made of the more 'precious' timbers such as oak, mahogany and red cedar. Some dining tables are built so that they can be extended when a big crowd comes to dinner; there are various mechanisms that allow the table to extend. Another method is the drop leaf style, where the ends of the table are hinged and fold down when not required.

Kitchen tables

Kitchen tables tend to get the most wear and tear of almost any surface in the house except the kitchen bench. Laminated surfaces work well because they handle the wear and tear, but if you prefer timber then this is fine too, especially with a polyurethane finish. From the art deco period of the 1920s and 1930s onwards kitchen tables took on a whole new personality, the new materials of the twentieth century allowing furniture makers to create tables of all shapes with new leg configurations such as central pedestals and all sorts of finishes.

Occasional tables

This term really covers all sort of tables that are used for this and that and can be easily moved for any need. The coffee table and the nest of tables common in homes through the middle of the twentieth century fall into this category. Occasional tables are normally quite small and often would have been made of oak or perhaps maple; however, nowadays they can be made of literally anything. Cane is a great material for the occasional table.

Wrought iron

Wrought iron is the type of iron work that is forged on an anvil. From earliest times the heated iron was hammered into shape. The hot metal is twisted, stretched and bent into plain or twisted rods, finials, scrolls, brackets, balustrades and hand rails. Recently, wrought iron has become a popular material for furniture, particularly kitchen chairs and tables. It is hard wearing and long lasting.

In the decorating scheme of things, you could say that soft furnishings are the final touch. But when you think about it, they really should be an integral part of the overall design of your home. It's not difficult to design cushions and other accessories to match the other elements, but if you have a large picture window, for instance, the curtains will be certain to make a major contribution to the overall decor. As always, the design rules of colour and space apply — the darker or brighter your curtains the more they will feature in the room, especially if they are against light-coloured surroundings. Correspondingly, curtains that blend in with the surroundings will make less of a statement.

Soft

SOFT FURNISHINGS AND FABRICS

Ginger is one of our family cats and he's a connoisseur of soft furnishings and fabrics! In fact he likes to road test them on a regular basis, as does his sister, Blossom.

When I think back to the homes of my parent's generation, I can't remember a single throw rug anywhere. We had a couple of cushions, but they were tiny and were purely for back support and were certainly not a feature.

Maybe it's because fabrics appeal to the woman in me, maybe I lived in a harem in a previous life — I don't know what it is, but I love this part of decorating and I love looking at pictures of sumptuous materials in gorgeous colours draped casually over simple furniture.

Soft furnishings and fabrics are the cheapest and quickest way to transform the look and feel of a room and there's no end to the variety of looks you can create — cosy country, Eastern exotic, cool and elegant, tribal and dramatic, whatever you want.

And in this area of decorating DIY is simple; anyone can make a bolster or pillow, hem fabric or sew on a tassel.

For the more adventurous do-it-yourselfer there are upholstery courses that can save you a lot of money in the long run. But if you don't want to go this far, it might be cheaper to find an expert to re-upholster your current furniture than to buy new pieces.

Bed linen ➢ blankets ➢ blinds ➢ curtains ➢ cushions and bolsters ➢ doonas, eiderdowns and quilts ➢ fabrics and fibres ➢ furniture covers ➢ lace ➢ lampshades ➢ pillows ➢ stains ➢ tablecloths and napkins ➢ throws ➢ leather ➢ upholstery

In the decorating scheme of things, you could say that soft furnishings are the final touch, the icing on the cake. But when you think about it, they really should be an integral part of the overall design of your home. It's not difficult to design cushions and other accessories to match the other elements, but if you have a large picture window, for instance, the curtains will be certain to make a major contribution to the overall decor. As always, the design rules of colour and space apply — the darker or brighter your curtains the more they will feature in the room, especially if they are against light-coloured surroundings. Correspondingly, curtains that blend in with the surroundings will make less of a statement.

In the bedroom, blankets, doonas, sheets, pillows and curtains are all very important decorative features that make up the overall style. Likewise, chair and couch upholstery and coverings can really help set the tone for lounge rooms, dining rooms and other recreational rooms. And then there are cushions. On a couch, chair, bed or the floor, cushions can be used everywhere and are one of the great items of soft furnishings.

Use soft furnishings to 'finish off' your decorating statement — there are a million things you can do. But, probably, the two most popular approaches are: whether to take a 'complementary' approach or a 'contrasting' approach. In making this decision you are really deciding on the statement you are going to make.

Bedrooms

Curtains, cushions, bedspreads, doonas, blankets, bed linen, fabric-upholstered chairs, throws, fabric lamp shades and those easy-to-do fabric-covered storage boxes are all soft furnishings that can make a huge difference to this most private room in the home.

Soft furnishings played an increasingly important part of bedroom decor — really, since societies moved from being nomadic to settling in one place. In ancient Greece, beds were often lavishly draped; in the 'bed chambers' of medieval Europe, curtains and canopies played important roles in decorating a room suitable for entertaining friends, as was the custom.

Today, we have a fantastic opportunity to draw on all the influences throughout history for our bedroom soft furnishings, whether they be from medieval Europe, northern Asia, the Pacific Islands or our own modern-day designs. Places like Bali with its intricate pattern designs in rich maroons, yellows and gold, the Pacific Islands with their colourful hibiscus patterns in sparkling reds, bright greens, sky blues and beaming yellows, and ancient Polynesian tapa motifs in earthy browns and blacks can be great for the Australian lifestyle, especially in the warm temperate and tropical regions. Moving south, there's a number of very Australian approaches — the 'beach house' look with its informal drapes and throws and the influence of the 'shearing shed' with its interplay between timber, corrugated iron and the rust, charcoal and grey curtain and upholstery fabrics. In the cool-to-cold climates such as Tasmania, the Victorian High Country, the Adelaide Hills and southern Western Australia, influences from colder areas of the Americas, China and Europe, such as quilting, have been adapted.

Bed linen

Bed linen was so named because sheets, pillow cases and towels were originally made of linen. However, once cotton was introduced, its strength, durability and ease of care meant that it soon took over as the most popular sheeting fabric. The popularity of cotton was further advanced through blending with polyester, which made it finer and softer and gave it a slightly silky feel. And, of course, polyester-cotton removed the need for ironing which made life even easier. Satin sheets, made from silk, are considered to be the ultimate bed linen (the cost is fairly 'ultimate' as well).

Bed linen comes in so many different colours and patterns these days that there's sure to be something to suit every decor. Choose from plain whites, florals, stripes, checks, all the primary colours and even blacks — and just about any combination in between. And with the more informal approaches, where bedspreads are less often used, the choice of sheets and blankets is even more important for the overall look of the room.

Washing bed linen

- Wash bed linen in hot water and, if possible, dry in full sunshine. The sunshine freshens, deodorises and sun bleaches the linen.
- Flannelette bed linen can be washed in the same way — but to avoid the fluff from flannelette do not spin dry. Instead, let them drip dry in the sun, which stops the nap (or fluff) from fluffing up.
- Beware of washing sheets with small tears in them — because of the weight of the water the fabric will rip further.

blankets and bedspreads

Blankets are a great decoration and design feature in the bedroom and can be used elsewhere in the home as well. A beautiful woolly, check blanket folded on a cane chair in the sunroom, with the soft winter's light filtering through the windows, will add warmth to a room. It's the same in the bedroom too; carefully chosen blankets not only keep you warm, they can change your bedroom from 'ordinary' to bright, gentle, colourful, restful or even sumptuous. When buying blankets, it's a good idea to think about the overall design and colour scheme of your bedroom and choose accordingly.

Bedspreads provide that neat, finishing touch over a blanketed bed and, depending on the style, they can be used to 'disguise' the bed during day time so, if you choose, with a few cushions and bolsters your bed can be turned into a couch. Today's bedspreads are becoming increasingly informal and, really, throws would often be a better description. Gone are the days of chenille, quilted satin and quilted velvet. Nowadays the most favoured solution is 'whatever works best is best', and this has created a great freedom in decorating styles for our beds. Choose from any materials you like: Indian cottons, luscious satins, country laces, contrasting checks, rich primary colours and florals are all popular, and you can use any combination of these. It can be great fun, and with a couple of hours' dabbling around in the remnant bins of your favourite fabric store, you could emerge with the makings of a beautiful bedspread.

Washing blankets

Here are some washing tips for blankets, but remember to read the maker's instructions first.

- Wash wool blankets with cold or tepid water using a wool wash detergent. They can be either machine washed or hand washed. However, be aware that large blankets can become very heavy once they are wet and therefore are difficult to handle.
- Synthetic blankets will not shrink, but to keep them soft and fluffy use a cold water wash. As a rule, try to dry blankets on a warm, windy day so that the air circulates through them.

Tips on looking after blankets

Blankets seem to be one of the few things these days that haven't been subjected to 'planned obsolescence'. They last and last — as long as they receive proper care. Here are a few tips to get those extra winters for your blanket dollar:

- If you put your blankets away for part of the year, make sure they are stored in a sealed plastic bag along with some moth repellent.
- Most blankets can be washed, but check the instructions on the manufacturer's label before you do.
- If you do decide to wash blankets yourself, it's a good idea to make sure your washing machine and clothesline can handle the size — they can be very heavy when wet.
- Pick warm, dry weather as getting large blankets dry can take some time.
- If you're unsure, take your blankets to a professional blanket cleaner — they have the equipment to handle these big woolly items.

Doonas, eiderdowns and quilts

Doonas, eiderdowns and quilts are essentially the same type of bedcover in that they all contain a filling such as down, a combination of down and feathers or a synthetic material, usually polyester. Traditionally they were filled with duck down or, to be more precise, down from the eider duck — hence the name 'eiderdown'. Eiderdown is now prohibitively expensive so a mixture of down and feathers from both geese and ducks is often used to reduce the cost. Alternatively, there are man-made fillings that, while not being quite as warm and toasty, do have the advantages of being washable and allergy free.

Another name for a doona is the 'continental quilt'; it was made popular in Australia through the immigration of many people from northern Europe during the second half of the twentieth century. The Australian-style doona has really copied the Scandinavian version — a big ribbed 'bag' of down and feathers that fits inside a cotton 'doona cover' which, in turn, comes in all sorts of colours and patterns. For beds with a box base, a matching or contrasting valance or 'skirting' is used to hide the none-too-attractive base and legs.

Eiderdowns and quilts are really the same thing — 'eiderdown' being the English terminology and 'quilt' being American. Eiderdowns have a number of coverings ranging from all sorts of inexpensive materials to lavish silks and satins, whereas the American quilt has developed quite distinctive design features of its own over time.

The subject of the American quilt, or the 'patchwork quilt' as it is often called, has been featured many times in a multitude of craft books and even in American novels and films. It had its beginnings with the seventeenth century migration of Europeans to the 'new world'. Of course, they took their eiderdowns and quilts with them for warmth and comfort and, as they began to wear, they patched them with whatever was available — material was in short supply in the early settlements. Then with the development of the cotton industry, instead of throwing away their old patched coverings in favour of fresh new cotton, the American quilt-makers seized on this abundance of new material to further enrich their established styles and designs — and quilts became part of American folklore.

Caring for doonas, eiderdowns and quilts

- It's essential with doonas, eiderdowns and quilts to follow the manufacturer's advice on cleaning.
- Generally speaking, down and feather-filled doonas, eiderdowns and quilts should be dry cleaned. (Washing can flatten the quilt and there is the danger that the fabric will rip, which will fill the washing machine with feathers!)
- If washing is absolutely necessary, very careful hand washing in cool water in the bath is advisable.
- Dry on a warm, breezy day that will quickly dry the quilt. Turn and shake the quilt a number of times to dry all the filling.

With quilts, doonas and eiderdowns you really have an endless number of decoration options — and ideas are as far away as the magazines in your local newsagent or the craft section of your local library. There was an interior design expert who once said words to the effect: 'You should just about be able to do a bedroom makeover by changing the bedding', and really you just about can.

Things to look for when deciding on doona covers are how you want them to go with the rest of the soft furnishings in the room. Are you after a certain style? You may like the colours and patterns to contrast, or you may prefer to opt for beautiful, soft creamy whites. You may like them to match the curtains or a fabric-covered box or you may like to have checks, stripes, florals and lace intermingling into a pot pourri of textures and colours. Whatever way you go, you'll have fun doing it and it's bound to look good.

And there's an added bonus in using doonas and eiderdowns and quilts on your bed — you can literally make the bed in 30 seconds!

Pillows

Pillows come in a number of shapes, sizes and materials depending on the culture from which they originated. Pillows filled with herbs and feathers have been popular throughout history for their relaxant and sleep-inducing powers; and in England pillows filled with dried hops have been used for centuries, the essential ingredient being lupulin, found in the fruit of the hop.

For the most part, the modern pillow is filled with one of the following: duck and goose down, down and feather mixtures, polyester or latex rubber. Pillow cases, or pillow slips as Mum used to call them, are usually purchased along with sheet sets and so match these but they don't have to. There's nothing to stop you having pillows of all sorts of different materials, patterns and colours to contrast with your sheets, blankets, doona or whatever.

Cleaning pillows

Polyester: Wash every few months to return their bulk and softness. They can be washed by hand or in a machine, but they need to be rinsed well and hung out to dry on a warm and airy day as they will take a very long time to dry in damp weather.

Latex rubber: Ideally, any marks on latex rubber pillows should be sponged off only. However, if the pillow does need washing, hand wash in warm soapy water and rinse several times.

Down and feather: It's not recommended to wash down and feather pillows. Take them to your dry cleaners and get some expert advice.

Bedrooms

Every bedroom has to have its personalised knick-knacks to make it feel lived in and give it something of your own special personality. All sorts of things fall into this category: mirrors, upholstered chairs, cushions, curtains, hat stands, dried flowers, tapestries, framed photos, paintings and fabric-covered jewellery boxes — to name a few. In fact, it's possible to turn a sparsely decorated bedroom into a cosy, private place with just a day or two's decorating. To do your research, grab some magazines — there are heaps at your local newsagent. Before you go out and spend lots of money, work out which items you can make yourself and which ones need to be purchased or made professionally. Curtains, cushions, picture framing, dried flower decorations, fabric-covered boxes and lamp shades are just a few of the many things that the average do-it-yourselfer can easily make.

Curtains and blinds

Curtains & blinds

Curtains are a very functional decoration for the home that provide privacy, control light and insulate the home against heat and cold, at the same time being an extremely important decorative feature. The perfect curtain would probably fulfil all these conditions, but this is often difficult to achieve. Some curtains, by necessity, are purely decorative and are never drawn across the windows. Others, such as muslin and net curtains, are used for privacy and decorative purposes but have little value as insulation. However, if possible, it is worthwhile considering the practical side of curtaining: used wisely they can save big dollars on fuel bills, keeping your home warm in winter and cool in summer.

Curtains can bring great style and sensuality to the home and, unfortunately for the insulation question, the modern trend is towards light, subtle, wispy curtains made of muslin, voile, sheer polyesters and various cottons that filter and dapple light or can be whisked across a window for privacy. In fact, contemporary interior decorators will often not dress a window at all, preferring to leave it bare. This is not always possible, of course, especially in houses kept true to an historic or cultural style. Here a Victorian or Edwardian home, for example, would demand formal drapes, just as a home designed and decorated in the Japanese style would require simple white translucent blinds.

Traditional curtains

In the nineteenth century curtains usually consisted of layers. The fine inner curtains were muslin or lace and were used to diffuse the light and screen the window. The curtains (or drapes) were often fixed at the top and so tie-backs were used to hold the curtains open. A 'valance', consisting of a piece of matching fabric, was suspended in front of the curtain to obscure the curtain rod at the top of the window.

There were many types of valances used to decorate windows and curtains. Throughout the nineteenth century 'festooned valances' were very popular, large swathes of fabric draped across the top of the windows and decoratively down the sides. The 'plain' (or flat) valance only became popular towards the end of the nineteenth century. It was first called a pelmet in the early part of the twentieth century and became simpler as the century wore on.

'Passementerie' describes the making of trimmings used to decorate curtains, valances and furnishings. These were trims such as cords wrapped in silk, woven or plaited edgings and tassels and fringes made from cotton and silk. In the mid nineteenth century, a valance was decorated with festoons of cords, fringes, tassels, ribbons and appliques of lace and velvet. One of the most popular fringes was the bullion fringe, where the threads were twisted around and wound back into the edge. It was so called because they resembled the gold officer's epaulettes.

Tie-backs too were decorative and elegant. They were made using silk cords, bows and fringed sashes and tassels in matching hues to the fabrics used in the curtains. Tassels were also used to decorate ornamental curtain rods.

In cottages and homes where the curtain rod was not concealed by a valance, the curtain poles were more decorative. They matched the wood colour used in the room or were metal or gilt with fancy finials (the decorative bulbs on the end of the curtain rods). In the nineteenth century the rods and finials became more and more decorative and were often embellished with festoons and crests. Carved and turned wooden finials were popular throughout the nineteenth century; rods and finials were also made of brass and iron.

Different curtains work better than others in different rooms. Lounge rooms are best with the more formal or sensual styles of curtains. Bedrooms often demand light-controlling curtains, while the children's room can look great with bright colours and animal or toy motifs.

One of the main aims with curtains is to make the window more attractive than it already is, and they can also change the apparent size and dimension of the

Traditional decorator fabrics still in use today

Buckram: Coarse linen or cotton used as a stiffener.

Burlap: Coarse plain fabric made of jute.

Broadcloth: Closely woven fabric with tiny crosswise ribs.

Calico: Plain woven cotton usually not dyed.

Chintz: Printed cottons, highly glazed to form a polished look.

Damask: Cotton and silk damasks are used widely for upholstery, curtains and covers. Silk damask is particularly thick and rich. It is a twill decorated with ornamental patterns that are woven into the fabric.

Gymp: Trim for furniture usually made of silk or cotton.

Hessian: Mixture of hemp and jute.

Holland: Type of linen used to cover chairs but also a term used to describe plain cotton roller blinds that are highly glazed so as to gather less dust.

Japara: Closely woven cotton used for cushions.

Marquisette: Gauze fabric that is loosely woven; used for curtains to diffuse the light and screen the window.

Muslin: Very basic plain woven cotton. Can be coarse or fine, dyed or unbleached.

Percale: Finely woven cotton. The higher the thread count, the better the fabric.

Plush: Fabric with a nap or pile like velvet but longer, usually cotton or silk.

Poplin: Heavier weight cotton with a fine rib.

Repp: Has a thick cord (or ribs) running across the width. Usually made of silk and wool.

Sateen: Cotton fabric woven with a satin finish.

Satin: Silk twill, glossy one side and matt the other.

Scrim: Plain lightweight cotton used for inner curtains.

Serge: Used in upholstery and made of silk or wool, it is a loosely woven twill and is very durable.

Silk: Includes watered silk, moire silk, satin, taffeta, organza, Chinese shantung and brocade — also raw silk (or Indian silk) sometimes called Tussore silk.

Tapestry: A fabric with a rich design forming part of the weave. Originally hand woven.

Twill: Fabric woven in a special way that is very strong.

Velvet: Fabric woven with a very short pile or nap, traditionally silk or a cotton-silk blend.

Voile: A crisp, sheer, lightweight cotton cloth.

Curtain tips

Placement: Generally speaking, it's best not to have a curtain sitting on the windowsill or touching the glass as they can become stained with dust from the sill and condensation from the window pane.

Fabrics: It's a good idea to buy only those curtain fabrics especially made for curtains. Curtain fabrics are designed and woven to drape properly. Using curtain or furnishing fabrics rather than ordinary dress fabrics can be a bonus because they are generally less likely to be affected by the sun's ultraviolet light. You may also find that furnishing fabrics may not be very colourfast when washing as normally they are rarely washed.

The sun's ultraviolet rays break down many fibres and cause fabrics to deteriorate. Cotton, linen, rayon, wool, silk and nylon are all subject to this. Polyester and acrylic fabrics are more resistant to light. Most furnishing fabrics are blended or have been treated in some way to protect the fibres from light. They may have special additives that absorb light or they may have coatings of polyurethane, rubber or silicone.

Patterned fabrics: Take care when purchasing patterned fabrics as the patterns may be difficult to match.

Lasting qualities: Light, breezy fabrics can look fabulous but it's also worth checking that they will withstand the ravages of sunlight, wind and damp — and if you're near the seaside, damp, salty air. This is where polyesters can be an excellent material.

Light control: Some curtain fabrics have a special backing that blocks out light. These fabrics do not need to be lined and are very good insulation.

Washing: Washable fabrics save on the expense of dry cleaning.

window. Narrow windows can be made to look wider by extending the drapes well beyond the window frame, or taller by keeping the drapes close to the window frame and hanging them longer than the sill. Windows that have an unattractive perspective, such as those looking out over a factory or wall, can be curtained with a lightweight lace or net that lets in the light but obscures the view. Tie-back curtains can be used to frame a picture window with a wonderful view.

Curtains can be gathered and pleated using special heading tapes and pins or curtain rings. A simple gathered curtain is usually achieved with a double drawstring pulled to evenly spread the gathers. Clusters of gathers can also be created with a second drawstring. Pencil pleats, cartridge pleats and pinch pleats use stiffened tapes and special hooks to achieve the desired effect. Recently, modern design trends have favoured a more casual approach to the way curtains are hung and gathered. Simple chrome and dowel rails, and even stainless steel chord, have replaced the formal curtain rail with its bulbous finials at each end. The curtains are then hung using all sorts of lightweight devices such as clips and rings where gathering and pleating occurs through the random position of the curtain and its supports rather than a precisely measured system of pleats and tucks. The more fabric you use the more pleats and folds you get.

Some curtains, especially those used for privacy or to mask an ugly view, are fixed and do not open and close. These are often sheer, net and lace curtains fixed to a rod or wire. To achieve a good effect of pleats and folds it's important to pay special attention to the width of

A safety consideration in the kitchen is to never have hanging drapes near cooking elements. Many curtains are made of flammable fabrics that can easily catch alight. Also, curtains over sinks will quickly become marked from splashes from the sink and steam rising. A blind is a more practical solution.

the material — three times the width of the window is a good rule of thumb. Some styles of curtains use more fabric, such as pinch pleats, and will therefore be more expensive, depending on the widths required. Curtains that do not have enough fullness can be a great disappointment, so it's important not to skimp on the width.

There are loads of different effects that can be created with curtains and each has its own most suitable fabric and style.

Caring for lace

Lace is very delicate and needs to be handled carefully. Just the weight of water can cause it to tear. Never use bleach on old lace — it will destroy the fibres of the threads. Wash lace curtains and throws or tablecloths inside a washing bag or pillow slip to protect them from abrasion.

Cleaning curtains

- Curtains are great dust collectors so, to keep maintenance to a minimum, it's a good idea to dust them often. Use the vacuum cleaner or a long handled brush.
- A good idea to freshen up curtains is to take them down and hang them outside on a sunny day with a light breeze. This will shake out dust and freshen the fabric.
- Many ready-made, lined and synthetic curtains cannot be washed successfully and will need to be dry cleaned. This may be an occasional cost but it is worth considering when you choose your fabrics.
- Curtains have to deal with dampness, wind, dust and sunlight and so keeping them looking fresh and clean is a challenge — as fabrics age they will lose their strength as the fibres break down, and if you wash a set of curtains that are starting to break down you may find they come out of the washing process in tatters.

Washing curtains at home

- The first rule for washing curtains at home is to closely follow the manufacturer's or supplier's instructions.
- Only wash washable fabrics like cottons, linens and man-made fabrics. Do not wash silk or wool or velvets or tapestries — have them professionally cleaned.
- Remove any hooks, undo the tapes and stretch the curtain tops out. You may be surprised at how large the curtain is — which might also change your resolve to wash it yourself.
- Give the curtains a good shake to remove the dust. Soak the curtains in cold water first in case they run. This should loosen the dirt too. Wash at a suitable temperature or, if you are unsure, wash in cold water. Make sure the detergent is fully dissolved before adding it to the water. Rinse gently and thoroughly.

Blinds

Blinds can be a great alternative to curtains, giving your window dressing options a considerable boost, and are good for privacy and light control but less effective as insulators. They can also work extremely effectively in tandem with lightweight curtains such as sheer polyesters, calico, muslin and other cottons.

There are four different types of blinds commonly in use — roller blinds, Roman blinds, Austrian or festoon blinds and Venetian blinds — and, of course, any amount of variations on those themes.

Roller blinds are the most common type of blind and, although they can be made in literally hundreds of different materials and styles, they most often use a bonded plastic material that is pretty much light proof. There are light-reflecting fabrics as well. Most common too are the spring-loaded rollers that allow the blind to be raised easily. Another advantage of roller blinds is that they come in a number of standard sizes and can also be made to measure, so they can always be fitted precisely and offer a really streamlined look. But the biggest advantage is the wide range of fabrics that can be used — you don't have to be stuck with plain blinds if you don't want to be. All sorts of materials and colours — satins, stripes, tapestries, floral prints, canvas, calico, liberty prints — can be used to create virtually any period of history and any colour match.

Roman blinds work on a 'pulley system' that usually raises the blind in deep, soft 'folds'. Materials can be wide ranging from translucent papers to calico and other plain cottons, to any variety of cotton prints. You can either go for plain colours to match the surrounding walls or you can go for something more contrasting that turns the blind and feature into something more prominent in the room. Roman blinds usually fit inside the window area and probably work best in a recessed window. But that's not a hard and fast rule either as they can work well in sections covering wide, full-length windows and doors, some being raised, some left lowered to block bright sun or a reflection to part of the room.

Festoon blinds, also known as Austrian blinds, are a gently 'cascading' type of blind that had its roots, as the name suggests, in Europe. They are similar in principle to the Roman blind but differ in the drape, which tends to fall at the edges creating a pleasant curve at the base of the blind when it is in the raised position. It's certainly a pretty look and would especially suit country and farmhouse styles and even Edwardian and the craftsman styles of the early 1900s. The fabric choice is pretty limitless, but a none-too-stiff material that will drape in a flowing fashion, or cascade, is most likely to give the best results. Some of the nicest examples are translucent enough to let light in while preventing seeing in or out.

Venetian blinds were all the rage back in the 1950s and 1960s when rock 'n' roll began and they certainly looked the part in the 1950s home. Venetians suddenly disappeared from view for about 20 years and then, just as suddenly, reappeared, possibly even more popular than before. Venetian blinds are the minimalist's choice of window dressing. Sleek, neat, easy to clean and made of a range of materials such as plastic, timber and steel, they come in many different sizes and colours, including a number of natural timber colours, and can be custom made to fit any window, even round ones. Apart from their great modern look and adaptability, venetians' great advantage is the way they can control light. The slats can be angled to allow light and sunlight to enter by just about any degree or they can be closed so light is kept out altogether. They're good insulators too and, in addition to their main use in lounge rooms, they are good for damp and steamy rooms in the house such as kitchens, laundries and bathrooms.

Cushions and bolsters

Cushions are definitely one of the most useful soft furnishings and probably the oldest too. Before chairs were invented, when human beings sat mostly on the ground, cushions provided them with some comfort, and they continued to do so even when chairs finally became upholstered many centuries later. Cushions still provide us with that service: on our timber, wrought iron and stone outdoor furniture; on unupholstered benches and chairs inside the home. Cushions on the floor can look great; you can line them up formally or you can simply gather a bunch of them on a rug in front of the fire on a cold winter's day, then settle down with a stack of magazines or a book.

Cushions come in a myriad of different shapes and sizes, textures and colours; the choices are infinite. You can make cushions out of just about any fabric too — tapestry, silk, linen, polyester, chintz, wool, Indian cotton, velvet, anything. Try cutting up an old Aran-knit woolly jumper and feature its textural design on the front of a richly coloured silk-backed cushion. On plain-coloured sofas, brightly coloured scatter cushions can give a room a lift. You can add lace for the bedroom, piping for the lounge room and borders for the kitchen. You can have round ones, flat ones, star shapes, sausage ones (bolsters), crescent shapes and seat cushions with ties. They can be striped, embroidered, patchwork, buttoned, check, floral, plain, leopard skin, spotted, anything at all.

There are four main fillings used in cushions: feathers, synthetic wadding, polyester filling, solid foam and foam chips. Foam (solid or chips) is great for outdoor use because that unexpected shower of rain won't do your cushions any harm. Dry them off, fluff them up and they're ready for use again. Synthetic wadding and polyester filling are both inexpensive man-made fillings that are probably the most popular these days. They have the advantage of usually being kind to allergy sufferers too. The number one filling for cushions, as it has been for centuries, is feather. Feathers are great because they have a long-living resilience and bounce back into shape with a simple 'fluffing up'. The natural things are so often the best.

Cushion maintenance

As with other fabrics and soft furnishings, it's just as important with cushions to make sure you're using the appropriate cleaning process. If you're unsure, get some professional advice to save disasters.

Feather: It's a good idea to give feather cushions an airing every now and then — choose a sunny day with a nice breeze. Washing feather cushions is not a good idea as it can take away the 'spring' in the feathers. It is much better to dry clean them.

Foam: Gently hand wash using warm soapy water and make sure they're well rinsed — several times. Try wrapping them in a towel to wring out all the moisture. Choose a nice warm day with a breeze to get them dry. Be careful not to dry them in front of a direct heat source as sometimes the heat will react with the foam to emit toxic fumes.

Synthetic: Machine or hand wash then dry on a warm breezy day. Be careful about dry cleaning — it might react with the filling.

Modern fabrics and fibres

The most commonly used textile fibres are cotton, linen, wool, silk, rayon, triacetate, nylon, polyester and acrylic. Here are their attributes.

FIBRE	DRAPE	LIGHT RESISTANCE	MILDEW/ MOTH RESISTANCE	APPLICATION
Acrylic	good	excellent	good	furnishings
Canvas	fair	fair	no	furnishings, blinds
Cotton	poor	will degrade	no	wide use
Linen	poor	will degrade	no	wide use
Nylon	good	fair	yes	general
Polyester	good	very good	yes	general
Rayon	good	fair to good	yes	silk look used in furnishings
Silk and satin	excellent	less than wool	no	used in blends
Triacetate	good	fair to good	yes	blends
Viscose	excellent	slow degrade	no	clothing
Wool	excellent	yellows and degrades	no	upholstery

Fabrics generally fall into three categories: natural fibres such as wool, cotton and linen; synthetic fibres such as acrylics, nylons and polyester; and blends such as polyester-cotton or polycotton.

Acetates

Acetate is not a strong fibre and does not absorb moisture well. It is often used to create fabrics that have the luxurious look of silk but the easy care of a man-made fabric. Acetate does not absorb moisture readily and dries quickly without shrinking. It drapes well and resists wrinkling. Triacetate is an improved acetate fabric that is easier to care for. Acetates can be hand washed in cool soapy water without rubbing and twisting. Rinse well and allow them to air dry. Press with a warm iron while still a little damp. Nail polish, nail polish remover, alcohol and various glues will melt acetate fabrics.

Acrylics

Acrylic fibres are produced from a petrochemical. Acrylics can have a wool-like and cotton-like appearance but are easy to wash and retain their shape well. It is often blended with wool and cotton. It is resistant to moths, oil and chemicals. It can be dyed in very bright shades and has a superior resistance to sunlight degradation. Acrylics usually will not need ironing and are best washed in luke warm soapy water.

Canvas

Canvas is a natural fibre with a course texture that is tough and resilient. Mostly it's used as the seating and backing for folding chairs, outdoor umbrellas and blinds — so it has to be tough. That's why it was used to make boat sails and tents. Certain weights of canvas are worth considering as curtains too.

Wash with soap or detergent and water, rinse thoroughly and stretch out to dry so that creases don't form.

Cotton

Cotton is a beautiful natural fabric that has so many uses it's hard to think what we would do without it. A versatile clothing fabric that breathes beautifully in hot weather, cotton is also great for all sorts of soft furnishings including curtains, cushions, bed linen, throws and upholstered furniture, where the coarser weave Indian cottons have tended to be the most popular in recent times. Cotton is also blended with various other artificial fibres to make stronger, longer-wearing fabrics where its natural feel and ability to retain dyes make it an ideal blending partner. Choose cotton for its strength, machine washable easy care and many weights and weaves.

Linen

Pure linen is made from the flax plant and is the strongest of the vegetable fibres. It has two to three times the strength of cotton and is lint free, which is why it was a popular choice for tableware. The lustre of pure linen is from the wax imparted from the plant. Pure linen wrinkles very easily, but like cotton it breathes. Linen is often blended with other synthetic fibres.

Net

These days net is usually made of polyester (or terylene) and often used for curtains and mosquito nets. Because it is draped over beds it can accumulate dust and quickly become discoloured. Net should be dusted frequently and can also be washed. Dry in the shade as sunlight will yellow the net.

Nylon

The term nylon refers to a family of man-made polymers. Nylon is exceptionally strong and weighs less than most fibres. Nylon fabrics are long lasting and resilient, the fibres are non-absorbent and dry quickly and are therefore suited to machine washing. Because the fibre is smooth, dirt does not cling to it. Wash nylon whites separately to avoid greying. Nylon melts at high temperatures so be careful to use only a warm iron.

Polyester

Try to avoid hanging curtains over a clothesline or they will get a clothesline mark. Put the pegs at each end of the curtains to form a large loop.

The most common polyester for manufacture into fibre is poly (ethylene terephthalate) or simply PET (also used to recycle drink bottles). Polyester fibres are strong, resistant to stretching or shrinking, quick drying, wrinkle and mildew resistant, easy to wash, and the fabric keeps its shape. Polyester and cotton are often blended to give a permanent press property. Polyester is also used for stuffing for pillows and upholstery because the threads wear well and are strong.

Rayon

Rayon is a manufactured fibre. It is generally made from natural cellulose fibre that comes from specially processed wood pulp. Rayon has many of the qualities of cotton, and is strong and highly absorbent. Rayon is a soft fabric that drapes well and is easy to dye. Most rayon fabrics should be dry cleaned, however, some can be washed but should not be wrung or twisted because the fabric can stretch when wet. Many velvets are made from rayon fibre.

Silk

Silk is one of our oldest textiles. During the Roman Empire silk was sold in return for gold. It is the strongest natural fibre, highly absorbent, cool in summer and warm in winter, it can be dyed easily to any colour and retains its shape and drapes well. All silk is washable but when washing silk do not wring. Silk dries quickly and should not be dried in a drier. Silk is weakened by sunlight.

Taffeta

Taffeta was once made of silk but now it is most commonly made of acetate, nylon, terylene or rayon and is often used for curtains, cushion covers and bedspreads. It can be hand washed and allowed to drip dry.

Wool

Wool is a marvellous material and it just goes to show that natural fibres can match man-made ones any day. Wool has some quite extraordinary features: it's hard wearing and resilient so it keeps looking good after many other fabrics would have had their day; it takes up dyes easily; its softness makes it a very comfortable fabric to touch and sit on; it naturally repels dirt; and it is fire resistant.

Woollen soft furnishings are best dry cleaned, but for small spills and spots sponge clean with a damp cloth. It's important too that your woollen fabric is moth proof; if not, it's a good idea to have it treated.

Lamp shades

Fabric lamp shades have been around for ages and are extremely popular in lounge rooms and bedrooms. Fabric lamp shades are a great rainy day do-it-yourself project and for minimal cost can add something special, especially when co-ordinated with other features in the room such as curtains, couches, carpets or bedspreads.

This is truly the domain of cotton and linen. Tablecloths were unknown in the western world until about the sixteenth century, when they were first used for wiping hands. The French used to have doubliers, a second cloth and often a longière, a third cloth for hand wiping. When napkins were first used they were more like towels and were hung from dining room walls.

Linen has long been the prefered fabric for tableware because of its strength, absorbency and hard wearing qualities.

Stains and how to deal with them

Here are some of the more common fabric stains and how to deal with them. When removing stains it is a good precaution to always test the solvent on an out-of-the-way corner of the fabric just in case it adversely affects the fabric. If in doubt, get the experts to help you.

Adhesive tape: Sponge with eucalyptus oil then wash in warm soapy water and rinse well.

Blood: For washable fabrics, soak in an enzyme solution before washing or soak in salted water. Otherwise tell your dry cleaner what the stain is so it can be treated accordingly.

Coffee: Sponge out in cool water. Rub detergent into the stain and wash as usual. If the stain remains stubborn, mix borax and hot water together to make a paste and rub it into the stain. Leave it to stand for about 30 minutes then rinse out the borax. Repeat if necessary.

Cosmetics: Dampen the stain and rub with powder detergent. Rinse and repeat if necessary.

Fruit stains: Fresh fruit stains can usually be removed if they are treated immediately. Sponge the stain with soda water. Rinse immediately and, if still there, rub in a powder detergent and rinse off. If this does not remove the stain, use borax and hot water mixed to a paste and apply this to the stain. Leave the paste on for 30 minutes then remove and rinse.

Greasy marks: For washable fabrics, wet the fabric and rub with a powder detergent, then wash as usual. Alternatively, rub with a pure washing soap in hot water then wash as usual. For dry clean only fabrics send to the dry cleaner.

Ink: Some inks can be washed out, but most will stain. Some are soluble in water, some in methylated spirits and others in acetone. Be careful that the solvent you use does not damage the fabric.

Mildew: First, try washing normally. If this does not remove the mildew spots soak in a household chlorine bleach solution of 1/4 cup bleach to 4 litres of cold water, then rinse. Alternatively, for a natural solution, rub with lemon juice and salt and leave in the sun to dry. You need to be careful that the bleach does not remove the colour in the fabric, in which instance it may be better to try a weak enzyme solution such as a nappy cleaner.

Paint: Paint stains are a bit of a catastrophe and therefore speed is of the essence. Try to clean up the paint stains immediately they happen. You have far more chance of removing the stain at this stage than later when it has dried. Read the label of the paint to see what solvent can be used. For paints with a turpentine solvent, dab the paint stain with a pad dampened with turpentine and gradually rub the area with the pad to soak up the paint. Wash and rinse as usual. For water-soluble paints rinse the fabric in water and rub the stain with some detergent and rinse. For paints that require expensive solvents, taking the fabric to a dry cleaner is probably the best solution.

Red wine: Great to drink, but hard to clean up. Sponge immediately with soda water or rinse with water and a little detergent. For washable fabrics, pre-soak in an enzyme solution before washing.

Rust: Here's another tough one to remove. However, there are some proprietary products available that will remove rust stains from certain fabrics. Test that the fabric will not be damaged first. A paste of lemon juice and salt applied to the stain and left in the sun will remove some rust marks.

Tea: As with most stains, it's important to deal with them immediately. If possible, flush the fresh tea stain with hot water — this should do the job. If the stain remains, make a paste of borax and hot water and apply to the stain. Dab off after about 30 minutes. Lemon juice and salt can also be used as an effective bleach.

Urine: Urine stains are easily removed if treated straight away. Rinse well and soak in an enzyme solution or one containing a powder detergent. Another method is to sponge the stain immediately with salty water. Old stains on sheets can be removed with chlorine bleach.

White wine: Although it might look like a harmless water stain, white wine will mature and oxidise with age causing yellowing and oxidisation stains. Sponge immediately with soda water or plain water with a little detergent, then rinse well.

Protecting your fabrics against stains

There are products available that help protect fabrics against stains. For example, stain-resistant acrylic carpets are made with sulphonated phenolic resins that have a high affinity to nylon. The stain-resistant agent provides an ionic barrier layer on the fibre surface that prevents acid dyes from penetrating into the fibre.

Fluorochemical products such as Scotchguard are resistant to both oil- and water-soluble stains. These products are best applied to articles that are seldom washed, such as upholstery.

Upholstery

It wasn't until about 250 years ago that upholstered furniture was invented. Until then we had to be content with a cushion on the hard wooden benches and stone seating. As the centuries went by, increasing amounts of padding were added to the seats, arms and backs of couches and chairs and they gradually morphed into the kind of upholstered furniture we know today. Horsehair was the main padding used by the early upholsterers, and the next major leap forward was the invention of the coil spring in the 1820s.

Slowly, modern styles of upholstered furniture developed and today we can choose from a multitude of styles: from those that take us back in history to the most sleek and modern. Construction has changed quite dramatically too, in keeping with the incredible advances in technology over the last 100, even 50, years. The traditional horsehair, cotton wadding and coconut fibre cushioning, held in place by hessian webbing, has now been replaced by various types of foam and synthetic fibres. The webbing is also synthetic nowadays and often specially tensioned springs are used. Restorers of antique upholstered furniture regularly use modern methods such as staple guns (which do much less damage than tacks) and nylon thread, which is many times stronger than natural yarns and will not rot or be eaten by moths.

Upholstered furnishings are usually covered in one of two ways: fitted covers and loose covers. Fitted covers are normally stretched tightly over the frame, which gives them a great tailored look. However, when they become soiled, they can be difficult to maintain as the covers

It's very easy to knit a beautiful blanket — lots and lots of 8 ply wool in any colour you like, 4.5 mm needles, cast on 40 stitches and knit squares in any or every pattern imaginable. A simple blanket stitch in a contrasting colour to join the squares together and you've got a heavy warm and much fought over blanket!

cannot be removed. For this reason darker fabrics are usually chosen to 'hide' any marks. However, dark-coloured fabrics can have a tendency to fade, so it's important to choose colourfast materials.

Loose covers, on the other hand, are draped over the particular piece of furniture. They tend to be light in colour and wear better than their fitted counterparts. Loose covers can look great as well with their informal and casual looks — and they have the great advantage of being easily removed for laundering.

Another option is to cover upholstered chairs and lounges with 'slip covers'. These can be made very formally and exactly or more informally depending on your inclination and budget. In one way it's a real pity to cover a beautifully upholstered chair or couch, however, slip covers have a number of advantages to offer:

- They protect upholstery against dust, stains and dirt — not a bad idea if you have small children.
- You may have a beautiful old armchair where the construction is still sound but the upholstery has seen better days. Re-upholstering is expensive and you may prefer not to take that option at this time. Instead you can make a slip cover for a fraction of the cost.
- Slip covers offer an easy, cost-effective way of redecorating. You can change the look of a lounge room quickly and easily and then change it back, if you like, at a later date.
- Slip covers can be whipped off in seconds and easily cleaned if made of laundry-friendly fabrics.

Slip covers can be made by the do-it-yourselfer who is a deft hand with the sewing machine, or they can be made to measure by a professional. Many people choose plain, light colours, but sometimes they can look a little too plain and formal and the slip cover ends up looking more like a dust cover. This is especially true of rooms where the period decoration of the home or the colour scheme requires something more colourful. Never be harnessed by the rules; take ideas and modify them to your likes, needs and lifestyle.

Upholstered furniture such as couches and armchairs are often quite large items. They take up a large area and therefore can dominate a room. It's a good idea to keep this in mind when you're purchasing a new lounge suite — make sure the size is okay and then, once that's worked out, make sure the colour you choose will work out in the whole context of your room. Remember, large items in a single colour can really take over and cause quite an imbalance.

This brings us to the issue of fashion colours. Getting a couch in the absolutely latest fashion and colours is a great experience — it can be quite euphoric. You smile to

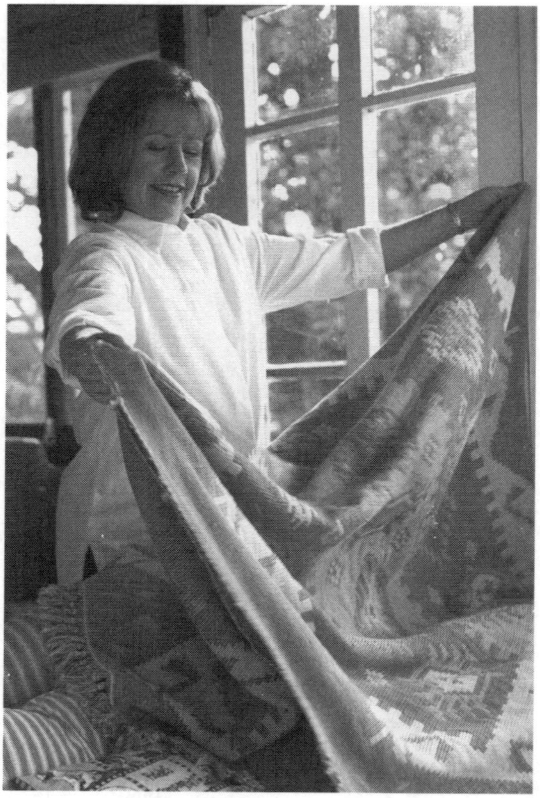

yourself: 'Hmm, this is fabulous, I couldn't be happier.' But a word of caution — fashions change quickly and upholstered furniture is expensive. And most of us can't afford to change our major furniture items like sofas or lounge suites very often. Bright and colourful can look ravishing when you get it, but after a while it can just as easily become irritating and can also make it difficult to change the look of the room at a later time. We all like to do a makeover of our main living areas as often as we can and the more unobtrusive the furniture is, the more you can change a room around. A good approach is that if you want some really bright and outlandish colours around the home, work with accessories such as cushions and curtains. It's a lot cheaper to change the cushion covers and drapes than to re-upholster the couch.

Throws

Throws really epitomise the current informal and relaxed approach to home decorating. They are most popular in bedrooms and lounge rooms, where they make great casual bedspreads and to toss across sofas, couches and armchairs of every description as a loose cover. Cotton is probably the most commonly used fabric, but there are plenty of other fabrics used as well. Thai and Indian silks make fabulously rich-coloured throws, and knitted patchwork wools can look beautiful as well.

Tips for lounge suites

- Consider the size of the room — a large room can take brighter colours and larger motifs, whereas a small room is better with small motifs and more subtle colours.
- Take care with bright, current-fashion colours and styles they mightn't be the best choice in the end. Look for something you can easily change and adapt.
- If you have children and pets, darker colours will stay fresh looking longer and a random print will not show up marks like a plain colour or a regular print.
- Darker colours need to be colour fast.
- Slip covers provide the answers to a lot of cleaning and decorating issues.

Leather

If you want your leather furniture to look great it should never stand up against a heater or be exposed to direct sun for any lengthy period.

Leather is one of the oldest forms of upholstery known. Most upholstery leather is either grain leather — smooth on one side and rough on the other — or full-grain leather where the grain side has not been made smooth. Modern upholstery leather has generally had special light-fast and anti-soiling treatments and does not need very much maintenance beyond regular dusting and vacuuming. It is advisable to add a bit of nutrition to the leather a couple of times a year; this should be done according to the manufacturer's instructions. Never use chemicals or synthetic detergents on leather.

Grease marks: Grease should be wiped off immediately with a paper towel or dry cloth. Grease marks will often disappear in time but for problem stains mix pure white soap flakes in tepid boiled water to make suds. Dab the suds on the leather with a lightly wrung soft cloth, then leave the suds to dry. Polish with a soft cloth.

Other stains: Stains should be dabbed, not rubbed. For water-soluble stains try to remove the stain by dabbing with clear, lukewarm water. Dab the entire leather surface at the same time. If this doesn't work, try the suds of white soap flakes as above.

Ballpoint pen ink: The ink settles in the raised areas of the leather. Roll a piece of paper towel into a point. Moisten the point with alcohol. Drag this along the pen line. Cut off the end of the point and repeat.

Scratch marks: Special repair dye can be used to cover up scratches. These dyes should be available from your supplier.

Upholstery tips

Enemies: One of the enemies of upholstery is direct sunlight. Its rays and heat can be magnified when it shines through windows, which intensifies the detrimental and deteriorating effects such as weakening fibres and fading colours. It's a good idea, if possible, to install blinds and curtains that shield your precious upholstered furniture from the sun when its rays are most harmful from mid-morning through to late afternoon.

Protective sprays: Protective sprays, such as Scotchguard, are a good idea for fabric upholstery. It protects the fibres from absorbing stains and dirt.

Dust and dirt: Vacuum upholstered items regularly as dust and dirt will stain fabrics and cause wear by weakening the fibres.

Spills: Remove spills immediately and sponge over to pick up any residue. Always treat spills straight away as even the most resilient fabrics can absorb stains and dirt given even a little time.

Stains: Treat stains with a damp sponge, working inwards from the edges so the stain is contained and doesn't spread further.

Upholstery shampoos: Shampoos are available for cleaning large pieces of furniture.

Professional cleaning: Every now and then it's worth having your upholstery professionally cleaned. Professional cleaners use special steam-based machines that are not unlike those used on carpets.

Dampness: Never over-wet upholstery. It's more than likely to leave a water mark or ring.

Leather: Leather can be wiped over with warm soapy water depending upon the finish on the leather. When purchasing a leather couch or chair make sure to ask the manufacturer what product will keep the leather looking at its best. Usually this would be a leather cream to keep it soft and supple and to prevent cracking.

Surfaces

SURFACES, FINISHES AND PRECIOUS THINGS

PUTTING THE FINAL TOUCHES TO YOUR HOME

I'm a great collector of ornaments, trinkets, souvenirs and general rubbish. Dusting it all is a nightmare. Occasionally I get fed up with it all and stick most of it into a cardboard box, but somehow it slowly builds up again.

As well as objects, my family has a tendency to find interesting things outside and bring them in to put on display. Currently inside we have about 50 cedar roses in bowls, a feather collection, lots of rocks, crystals and shells picked up from our travels, a vase full of dried autumn leaves, another with dried banksia, a bird's egg — and that's just off the top of my head!

My children began their education in Steiner schools and they had a wonderful idea that we copy from time to time: a nature table, like a little altar, that was draped in coloured muslin and decorated with an aromatherapy oil burner and candle, some rocks and crystals, a bough from a tree that reflected the season i.e. bare in winter, blossoming in spring etc. There was also a vase of something available in the garden, pine cones and often some little knitted animals or clay figures to represent fairies or elves.

The boys are very observant of nature and its changes through the year and I think it's simply because of this focus on what's happening around them.

It's difficult for city children to feel connected to the earth without this kind of experience, so making the effort to show them is really worthwhile. It's good for the spirit to recognise and appreciate beauty in all its forms.

CHOOSING A SURFACE FINISH

Aluminium ➢ granite ➢ benchtops ➢ brass ➢ ceramics ➢ china ➢ chrome ➢ copper ➢ corrugated iron ➢ enamels ➢ glass ➢ laminates ➢ marble ➢ melamine ➢ pewter ➢ porcelain ➢ shelving ➢ silver ➢ stainless steel ➢ tiles ➢ timber ➢ tin ➢ vinyls

Choosing the right surface finish for benchtops, shelves and cupboards can be a real conundrum — but it needn't be. Follow our 'golden decorating rules': spend time in the room, do your research and costings and, if you're still in a muddle, get some professional advice.

Your choice of finish for a benchtop, a bathroom vanity or built-in wardrobe, for example, can depend on a number of considerations, especially if there is a special feature you would like to keep, like an old free-standing bath, an island workstation in the kitchen, or mum and dad's special porcelain complete with display case. Just take your time; you're presumably going to live with your decision for many years. Consult books and magazines, make notes of things you like and eventually a solution will come — maybe sitting bolt upright at 3 am in the morning, but it will come.

Bathrooms

Rooms don't come any wetter, damper or more humid than the bathroom. In an average family there are at least four showers or baths daily creating an atmosphere like a Swedish sauna, not to mention the numerous other visits. Water gets splashed, trodden, flicked, dripped and spilt everywhere. And what about our little favourites — the nightly bath can be close to a war zone with Lego aeroplanes and spacecraft dive-bombing the water as if it's Armageddon; or beautiful dolls being bathed, with their latest fashion accessories being hung out to dry over the side of the bath. Funny, but whatever the game, water always ends up everywhere. However, within certain limits bathtime is a wonderful opportunity for play and a

Tips on aluminium

Aluminium was often used around the edges of timber and laminated benchtops and, of course, for pots and pans. It is a very soft metal, easily dented and tarnished, and easily eroded by various cooking liquids and other kitchen substances. Generally speaking, it has been superseded by stainless steel, a far more stable product. However, for those of you who still have bits and pieces of aluminium about, here are some tips.

- Do not to leave food overnight in an aluminium saucepan as it can react with the metal and leave pits, not to mention the metal reacting with the food!
- To restore a tarnished aluminium pan, burnish the surface with a plastic scouring pad or fine steel wool.
- A green method for discoloured pots and pans is to boil up a weak acid solution — try some lemon rind or rhubarb.
- Aluminium fittings should be wiped with a damp cloth then waxed. Don't use abrasive cleansers or pads.

great way to unwind at the end of the day, so it would be churlish to curtail any creativity.

All this means that when you think bathroom, it's essential to think waterproof. A bathroom has to function properly both for day-to-day operation and good hygiene. On the other hand, we all want our bathrooms to look great too, so with functionality must come good, stylish looks. Fortunately, with the abundant finishes available to us it's easy to achieve.

Like any other room in the house, the bathroom is an expression of yourself and your lifestyle. A couple without kids, for example, would not require the same safeguards against wetness, nor would the eligible bachelor (we hope) nor the parents whose kids have grown up and have families of their own. (Watch out, though, when you're landed with the grandchildren!) A bathroom in tropical regions should ideally be open and airy, whereas in cooler temperate climates it's cosier if the bathroom is enclosed and warmed against the winter cold.

The most popular finishes in the bathroom are ceramic tiles for the walls, floors, showers and edgings, vitreous china for toilets and basins, and acrylic or porcelain-enamelled steel for baths. It can be a great look and super easy to clean, but you don't have to be a slave to the ceramic tile if you don't want to be — and there are thousands of homes that are on your side.

When decorating, look at various basic design styles and finishes, just as you would for any other room in the home. Have a think about these options:

- black and white
- bold, dynamic colours
- classical
- fabric and wallpapers
- mediterranean
- minimalist, futuristic
- mirrors
- pastels
- rustic or country-style.

First, look at the present character of your home or, if you're building a new home or renovating, look at the overall style you have chosen. Your bathroom should reflect the general design style. If your look is sleek and modern, go for that; if it's an Edwardian or art deco home, keep those essential design features, even if you are taking a more modern approach.

Take care to keep costs in mind when redecorating or renovating — when you start altering the plumbing the project can become very costly. Try to spend your budget on the things that really matter; that is, the things that are really going to make a difference. You might like to prioritise these by writing them down in order of importance. Here's a checklist of the basics:

- fixtures
- floor
- heating and cooling
- lighting
- who are the main users?
- safety
- storage
- ventilation
- walls

Be very very careful about mates and families working on your house. Close relationships have been known to sour over verbal agreements that have gone wrong and misunderstandings over when, what and how things are to be done.

It may be cheaper to do things yourself, but it's still worth getting quotes from qualified, recommended trades people just to compare.

I'm not suggesting you need a written agreement if you're using friends and relatives, but it's certainly worthwhile putting everything that's been agreed down on paper to avoid later tensions.

Check your priorities against your budget, making sure that any potential or current problems, such as dampness, are well covered. Now it's time to do your research. Check out magazines and architectural or interior design journals at a good newsagent or library. Bookshops that specialise in design books can be a great source of inspiration; and you can consult an interior designer or your local building centre. There are heaps of brochures, too, you can get from manufacturers and bathroom centres.

Scribble down some thoughts on what you'd like to do, some rough sketches or plans. You may have an old-style vanity that you want to replace with a sleek, new free-standing basin. This, in turn, may reduce your storage and make your shower and bath look out of place and old-fashioned — and you may decide on a whole new minimalist look. You may want to decorate your bathroom in a country style, with cane chairs, dried flowers, wallpaper and timber panelling. It's all possible. Sort through your ideas, work out your vision and sketch it out.

Think about how you use your bathroom. Are you a great lover of long hot bubble baths? If so you may well want to create a relaxing room that you can enjoy. If it has a private view or looks out on a private courtyard, you may like to make use of that as part of your overall bathroom environment. Some trees and shrubs outside the window may make a great difference and, in summer, large windows could actually be opened to the view or courtyard. Alternatively, it may look directly out on the neighbour's kitchen window — whoops! — in which case curtains, venetian blinds or one of the many translucent glasses is probably the answer.

Textures and patterns are great in bathrooms too — a quirky line of tiles down the centre of the room; curtains and wallpapers used to give a gentle 'cottage' effect; the gleam of clean white ceramic tiles or charcoal-coloured marble for a smooth futuristic look; the textural depth that can be achieved by the clever use of mirrors; the rich honeyed patterns of pine and other timber panelling; a blend of painted timber panelling and painted walls and furniture (a great look and inexpensive too); paint and stencils — the list is as long as your imagination.

The great thing is that you don't have to spend a bomb to make your bathroom look good. More often than not the layout is fine; it's the fittings, the bath, the toilet seat and so on that have become a bit tired and worn. Things like baths can often be resurfaced, and if you have one of those beautifully made enamelled-iron baths, why not? Most likely you'll be able to change the colour as well. Check with your local building centre for reputable companies and their services. So with a coat of paint, a bit of regrouting on the tiles, some new taps and fixtures, some fresh ideas for the lighting and some resurfacing work on the bath and basin, you could have a bathroom that looks like new — and it will keep its original look.

Bathroom green tips

We live in a dry country that's always short of water. We can help alleviate Australia's water shortage quite dramatically by sensible everyday water usage in the bathroom.

- Make sure the taps don't leak and are properly turned off.
- Install dual flush cisterns and water-saving shower roses.
- Turn off the tap while brushing your teeth.

Damn the damp

Anything that suffers from as much consistent moisture and humidity as a tropical rainforest is going to cause you problems unless, like mother nature, you can give it a good airing. With bathrooms, you need to ensure that water and splashes aren't going to disappear into seams in the walls or floor and that water can drain away easily. Once water gets into the woodwork or under floors your problems begin. Watch out for badly sealed showers and leaking taps; these are usually simple problems easily solved, but need to be taken into account in your decorating priorities. Ease of cleaning is also important. Along with the kitchen, the bathroom is the other room in the house that needs the most cleaning — and you want it to be as easy as possible. Fiddly nooks and crannies make for hard work; simple shapes and surfaces of water-sealed materials make life easier. Another most important item is ventilation; if your windows can't do the job properly, install an exhaust fan to get rid of humidity as it occurs and create a draught for air movement through the room.

Bathroom basins and vanities, baths, showers, toilets

Basins and vanities

After decades of bathroom basins being enclosed in 'vanity units', the wheel has turned forwards (or come full circle if you're old enough) to free-standing basins on pedestals or mounted directly onto walls. Their advantage is they create a feeling of space, are easier to clean and don't provide 'pockets' of damp like the cupboards and drawers of vanity units. However, they don't solve storage problems.

New looks, materials and surfaces provide all sorts of solutions for vanities. Benchtops have taken on a 'chunkier' look and now come in an amazing array of colours, shapes and sizes to suit any bathroom from the largest to tiniest cupboard. And there's a huge range of benchtop materials available for bathrooms and kitchens — laminates, granite, marble, limestone (both must be sealed) and terrazzo are all popular.

Basins, like toilets and baths, are mostly made of vitreous china, enamelled steel or enamelled cast iron to create hygienic, easy to clean surfaces. Today's options are endless and can be tailored to just about every taste and budget. Your nearest bathroom centre is a good place to lose at least half a day.

Baths

The bath is one of the most welcoming and functional fixtures in the home. It's a focus of family life, serving all the family from the very young to the elderly. It's where we bathe with the newborn baby, where the kids have their nightly clean up and fun; it's a remedy for those aches and pains after the football match or hiking trip; and it's a little piece of luxury where you can soak away for hours on end while devouring your favourite novel.

Although the tiled baths of Roman times would have taken some beating, the best baths are made of enamelled cast iron, much sought after and still available. Nowadays baths are generally made of enamelled steel and fibreglass-plastic materials. Modern technology, too, has provided a vast range of different shapes and colours to choose from; and for the ultimate piece of pampering there is always the spa bath to gently massage and soothe the body and mind.

The height of a bath, whether it is sunken or standard height, and whether it is enclosed or free standing, can make a big difference to the overall look of a bathroom. The sunken bath with wide, low, tiled steps up from the floor can help create the Roman look, either classical or sleekly modern. Most baths these days are tiled on the exterior to make a completely sealed unit, easy to clean and no doubt providing some insulation to keep the water warm. Changing from tiles to timber will give you a completely different feel again — mainly 'Swedish sauna' or 'country'. Again the options are countless.

Showers

Most people have recessed showers, tiled to match the rest of the bathroom. The 'recess' requires only a glass door or curtain to prevent water splashing everywhere. Alternatively, the whole unit can be made of toughened glass or fibreglass and there are some beautiful designs available — sometimes framed in enamelled aluminium or chrome but, with the advent of strong and safer toughened glass, they are more often frameless. If your bathroom is small the best solution may be to place the shower over the bath. Of course, you can plan your bathroom's drainage system so that you need no shower recess at all — water splashes about but quickly drains away which is a great solution for warmer tropical climates. But for the rest of us, especially if you have decorated your bathroom in moisture-absorbing materials such as wood, the shower needs to be separately partitioned off and well sealed.

Measure up, measure up and measure up again. Buy your fixtures and fittings before you start building or renovating and check the dimensions several times to make sure you don't end up with a fridge that won't fit the hole, or a sink that won't accommodate the brilliant taps you've just seen. If you don't buy everything upfront, you may find the oven you wanted in the brochure is no longer available or the wrong size.

Taps, shower heads and other fixtures

Here is where you have the most astonishing array of choices including that wonder of modern technology, the hands-free tap, which along with thermostatically controlled taps represent great technological leaps forward in modern tapware.

Taps are an integral part of any bathroom design, yet they are often the last thing chosen. Taps are not cheap, so it pays to take time and care choosing them. They are important to the overall look of the room and need to be compatible with the basin, bath or shower.

The standard issue is separate hot and cold taps, but there are also single action mixer taps and mixers with

There's a wonderful array of decorative bath plugs to choose from now — they've become an art form, and they're certainly easier to pick up underwater than the common garden variety plastic plugs — just be careful you don't sit on them if they've got bits that stick out!

separate controls. Finishes include the very popular chrome, ceramic, enamel in various colours, brass, gold plate and acrylic.

If you don't want a complete bathroom renovation you can really make a difference to your bathroom by simply changing the furniture and accessories. Things such as taps, shower roses, shower shelves for shampoo and soap (secured by screwing through the tiles), toilet seats, toilet roll holders, mirrors, shelves (glass ones look great), towel racks and toothbrush holders can all help give a new look to the room. You can choose a style for the accessories that changes the whole look of the room. Glass can look great, even for towel racks; timber and granite do too. And don't forget the humble plug — it adds that finishing touch. There are some very decorative ones available.

Green cleaning tips for the bathroom

You can clean your bathroom with commercial cleaning products, but why not try these environmentally friendly tips:

Bath 'rings': try rubbing with bicarbonate of soda on a wet rag or sponge. Vinegar is another option.

Chrome taps: wipe with soapy water then wipe dry, or rub with methylated spirits until shiny.

Benchtops — good ideas for surface finishes

There is a marvellous range of benchtops and worktops available to suit just about any need. A kitchen benchtop has to take heavy wear and tear and be water and stain resistant, as well as look stylish; whereas the bathroom benchtop doesn't normally need to be so tough but, above all things, it needs to be water resistant.

Please note that if you choose limestone or marble, even if it's sealed, then perfume drips and toothpaste will need to be wiped off quickly.

For information on benchtops and worktops look in the Yellow Pages under each of the materials; and you'll find useful information about the various materials' qualities in other chapters as well. This list gives an idea of the huge number of choices available:

- laminates
- timber
- marble
- limestone
- stainless steel
- terrazzo (a mixture of glass or marble chips set in concrete and epoxy resin)
- granite and flecked granite
- ceramic tiles
- slate.

Brass

Brass is still a popular finish, especially for fittings such as door handles, cupboard and drawer handles, window latches and sometimes as taps in country-style kitchens and bathrooms. Brass is an age-old metal substance, a mix of tin and copper, and is rust proof and hard wearing.

Often brass fittings are lacquered to stop them from tarnishing, in which case cleaning is easy. Merely wipe over with a damp cloth; some experts suggest rubbing a little silicone wax onto the fitting occasionally. If the lacquer becomes worn or scratched, it's best to remove it using a commercial lacquer stripper and then reapply a fresh coat. Another option for stripping lacquer off brass is methylated spirits or nail polish remover.

Unlacquered brass can tarnish much like other metals. You can used a commercial brass polish or any number of homemade remedies. The advantages of the homemade ones are that they are cheap and easy, you don't have the inconvenience of having to go to the hardware store, and they're often kind to the environment. Try the green tips below.

Green tips for unlacquered brass

- Rub the brass fitting with a paste consisting of salt, vinegar and a little flour to bind it altogether. Allow to dry, then clean off with a damp cloth and polish.
- For engraved or pitted brass try scrubbing with an old toothbrush and household ammonia. Toothpaste can work too.

Ceramic artefacts, porcelain and crockery

NONI SAYS

My children are naturally quite careful and in shops when they were young they could be trusted not to break anything. I let them pick things up and examine them knowing it was highly unlikely that there would be an accident. This caused several shopkeepers considerable anxiety over the years, an understandable attitude when you see people who are like bulls in china shops.

Accidents happen and precious objects do get broken occasionally — but it's no use crying over spilt Ming!

A friend of mine was washing the dishes for me one night when Charlie was a baby and she accidentally broke his bunnykins cup, a present from one of the women who was at his home birth. In other words, it was a reasonably precious object. Her immediate reaction was to freeze with a horrified expression on her face, then she started to gasp and sob. I wasn't upset in the slightest and told her so and hugged her because she was so distressed. When she was a child her mother had gone berserk if she'd broken anything, giving her a belting and putting her in her room.

The bottom line is that people are more important than things. If objects are irreplaceable they shouldn't be placed where they're at risk.

Who has got their great aunt's Royal Doulton dinner service, that she received on her wedding day, safely packed away in the cupboard; or grandmother's beautiful Wedgwood or Staffordshire ceramic vase tucked away in a safe corner of the loungeroom? It's wonderful to have objects that are special to you to enhance a room or to bring out for special occasions. There are lots of different types of ceramics from any number of different countries all around the world.

Ceramics generally fall into two categories. The first is low-fired pottery or earthenware and soft-paste porcelain, which tend to be quite porous and fragile. Examples of this pottery are Majolica and Indian pottery. Bone china is the most common example of soft-paste porcelain. The second category is high-fired stoneware or pottery and hard-paste porcelain which tend to be durable and non-porous. Things like Dresden (Meissen) porcelain from Germany and Chinese porcelain fall into this category.

Crockery and ceramics should last a lifetime or more and are quite resistant to everyday environmental effects. However, continual use of items such as teapots, which are subject to constant moisture and heat, will gradually take its toll. So, if you've got a special item, try to prolong its beauty and use it only on special occasions.

Apart from dropping them and knocking them over, crockery and pottery are pretty hardy. Porous objects do absorb moisture, which can cause discolouration and swelling, while glazes can succumb to hairline cracks known as 'crazing'. A dry heat and stable environment is the best way to minimise damage.

Stacking special crockery needs to be done carefully to preserve it. Odd-sized plates and dishes should be kept separate and, as the bottom rims of ceramic plates are often unglazed, it's a good idea to make up some felt pads to sit between them.

Ceramic tiles

See also under 'Floors' on page 52 and 'Walls and ceilings' on page 94.

Ceramic tiles are immensely popular in the home. They're used for floors, walls, bathroom surrounds, benchtops and, of course, they're used extensively outside the home as well. Here we will deal with them in their role as finishes on benchtops, where they are not quite as

The dos and don'ts of cleaning ceramics and porcelain

Be very careful when washing precious ceramics and crockery and get expert advice before using any detergents and cleaners on your special items.

- Wherever possible, dust rather than wash.
- Avoid the dishwasher; this is a big no-no. Many special pieces are not dishwasher proof.
- Porous objects should not be immersed in water. If dusting will not clean it, use a slightly damp cloth but be very careful of cleaners and detergents, which can cause discolouration, leaching and damage to decorative work.
- Don't immerse objects decorated with gold and silver in water and detergent solutions. Gold and silver decorations are often added after the glaze and are very susceptible to cleaners and rubbing.
- Keep liquids that stain, such as coffee, away from your precious ceramics.
- Don't wash ceramics with aluminium pots and pans — it can cause a grey stain.
- When washing ceramics and crockery use as little detergent as possible and make sure the water is warm, not hot. Hot water can cause the little hairline cracks called 'crazing'.

If you're like me and you lack confidence about making tiling a feature on a larger area of wall, then take advantage of the little splashback area of your sinks, basins and cooktops. You can go mad on colour and design here and if you look around you can find some stunning individual feature tiles. Craft markets and antique shops often have a collection of one-offs or limited sets that you can use as the basis for your masterpiece.

popular these days, and splashbacks, where they are extremely popular.

Ceramic tiles provide quite a different style of finish to other benchtops as, unlike laminates and stone slab, they are segmented. This, of course, is caused by the fact that ceramic tiles have to be laid with a thin section of grout between each one to allow for expansion as they age; and the trick is to get a smooth, even surface so when you put down your glass it doesn't topple over. (People could get the wrong idea about you.)

However, tiles on benchtops can look extremely effective and make a fabulous contribution to the look of a room. In the kitchen, terracotta is probably the most widely used. It can provide an added dimension to a rustic or country style. Alternatively, you can try other colours and textural effects such as highly polished glazes in anything from creams through to charcoals. But whatever you do, don't drop a plate on a tiled benchtop — it will be curtains for that dish. Tile sizes vary, but something around 200 mm^2 is fairly normal.

In the bathroom, ceramic tiles are much more common as benchtops and the huge variety means you can do just about anything. Try little glass (mosaic) tiles on a benchtop, or any of the extraordinary range of plain and patterned tiles available. Don't disregard the notion of tile benches in the laundry either, where they can look great and offer a really functional surface.

Splashbacks, those areas in kitchens and bathrooms behind sinks and stoves and baths and vanities, are where the ceramic tile comes into its own. Here you need something stylish, but something that is easy to clean — after just about every meal you have to wipe around the stove or behind the sink. And what makes them such a popular choice, apart from their ease of cleaning and durability, is the absolutely enormous range of colours, shapes, patterns and textures available. Now, this is one part of home decorating where your head might begin to spin; but if it does, just come back to your original vision.

Splashbacks are a great opportunity to really stamp your mark on the look of a room, because of it being a limited area. Think about all the border and frieze tiles available, not just in patterns and colours but in shapes as well. You may like to intersperse large and smaller tiles — many larger tiles are manufactured with the corners cut off to allow little tiles to be inserted. These small tiles can be matching or a contrasting colour, or they can be patterned. You may like the classic borders and friezes of yesteryear, or you may prefer the modern stark white approach. Whatever you choose, you'll have a good time doing it because there are ceramic tiles to suit every style and budget.

China

Cleaning fine bone china is essentially the same process as cleaning ceramics and porcelain. Be very careful about which detergent you use and its strength: the less the better. Wash precious objects in warm, rather than hot, water; the heat can cause hairline cracking.

Now if you bump or drop your favourite china setting, it's a pretty safe bet that something will at least chip or break. The diehard do-it-yourselfers do repair precious items, but really it's a job best left to the experts. Often, your local antique store can recommend a conservator or craftsperson; and try the major art galleries in each state, state libraries and museums as well. They sometimes have conservation departments who will often give you valuable advice.

Chrome

Chrome is a great finish for taps, door and cupboard handles, window latches, edgings and various features in the kitchen and bathroom. It is produced by electroplating and chromising. Electroplating takes two forms: decorative plating which is usually used on nickel; and 'hard' plating, which is very wear resistant.

For cleaning, take care not to use abrasive cleaners or cleaning pads as chrome is easily scratched. Try these solutions for cleaning chrome:

- window cleaner
- methylated spirits
- household ammonia
- non-abrasive household cleaners.

For chrome that has rust marks or other stubborn stains, try a non-abrasive silicon car polish. Chrome that is in contact with a lot of moisture in the bathroom or near exterior windows and is susceptible to rust can be cleaned by first polishing with methylated spirits, then wiping it over with a thin film of petroleum jelly.

Copper pots and pans

Copper is often preferred by professional chefs for their cookware because of its ability to conduct heat quickly and evenly. Nowadays, these excellent quality pots and pans are available to all of us and, because they are used for food preparation, it is very important that you don't use cleaning agents on them that are in any way dangerous to your health.

Copper will tarnish and needs to be given a good polish from time to time. If you choose a commercially available cleanser make sure it is safe for using on cookware. Home-made cleaners are great because they are cheap and easy to make, and are often kind to the environment as well.

Take care with acid substances such as lemon juice and vinegar; if too concentrated or left on too long, they can react with the copper, causing pitting. Make sure you wash and dry the pot thoroughly before putting it away.

Homemade cleaners for copper pots and pans

- Calcium carbonate (whiting). Make a paste with a little methylated spirits and water.
- Rub on a paste of equal parts of salt and vinegar mixed with a little flour. Allow to dry, then polish off and rinse thoroughly.
- Rub with a solution made up with one tablespoon of salt and two tablespoons of vinegar. Rinse the pan in warm soapy water and dry.
- Make a paste of buttermilk, lemon juice and a little flour. Rub onto the pan and allow to dry. Then polish off, rinse thoroughly and dry.

Enamel and enamelware

Most stoves, fridges and washing machines have an enamel or enamel-like finish, but apart from these sorts of appliances, enamel seems to be a less popular finish at present than it was, say, twenty years ago. Maybe it will come back, because it can have a great look. Stove elements, enamel baths, colanders, jugs and those wonderful enamel mugs we always took camping are usually coated with what's called vitreous enamel — a glass fused to metal. Try these enamel tips:

- Whether it's vitreous enamel or the sprayed on enamel, these finishes are susceptible to scratching, so be careful not to use abrasive cleaners and scouring pads.
- The best cleaners are normally the simple spray-on household cleaners — spray on, wipe off, then do a final wipe with a damp cloth or towel.
- For stubborn stains try a cream cleanser, but take it gently.
- To prevent the white film forming on enamelware, try drying them immediately after washing.
- One of the annoying things about enamel is that it sometimes chips, but luckily there are products that can fix these sorts of accidents easily. Get some advice on the latest products from your local hardware store.

Glass

Remember the old-fashioned glass-topped coffee tables so often with a crack? That particular hazard is long gone and glass has entered a new era with safer fabrications and styles.

Now, newer, tougher glass can be used almost anywhere in the home — as benchtops, featured space dividers, super-tough tables, shelving, cupboard doors and various other fittings and knick-knacks.

Types of glass

Annealed: the standard, average glass normally used for windows and available in various thicknesses.

Heat-strengthened: generally twice as strong as annealed glass of the same thickness and configuration, this glass has been subjected to a heating and cooling cycle to give it extra strength. Heat-strengthened glass is intended for general glazing such as windows where some additional strength is required.

Laminated: commonly called 'safety glass', it is actually two sheets of glass with a resin or plastic sandwiched in between. Generally it is the thickness of two standard sheets (just over 6 mm), however, it is also available in a variety of thicknesses and colours and may be mirrored, sandblasted or stencilled. The sandwiched plastics and resin can be varied to achieve a desired effect; for example, a plastic can be used to give a rice paper effect, or a resin can give a strong colour like red. Laminated glass can be broken but does not fracture into pieces, instead remaining largely intact because the broken sheet still adheres to the 'sandwich'. It is not resistant to heat. Laminated glass is used in many safety applications in the home where broken glass shards would be hazardous — for splashbacks around benches in kitchens (but not around stoves because of the heat), in bathrooms, for banisters and verandahs.

Tempered glass: this glass is up to five times stronger than annealed glass of the same thickness. It is toughened through a special process of heating and cooling and when broken shatters into many small fragments roughly cubic in shape. Tempered glass is more flexible and more resistant to heat, which means it can be used in many places throughout the home — vanity tops, benchtops, tabletops, splashbacks around stoves, sliding doors, storm doors, building entrances, shower recesses, interior partitions and wherever superior strength and safety properties are required. Tempered glass looks stylish as well as being functional and is simply cleaned with window cleaner.

One of glass's greatest attributes is its transparency which, in turn, can create a great sense of depth, space and light in the home. Ironically, its other major attribute is that it can be translucent and opalescent as well, creating plenty of fascinating effects, all actually plays on light. Frosted and etched glass, with their varying degrees of translucency, can provide great solutions for kitchen and bathroom cupboard doors. The misty forms of the objects within can be seen from the outside and there is plenty of light available inside. The milky and distorted iridescence of opalescent glass with ribbed and patterned finishes can somehow create an impression of fluidity and movement. And there are plenty of talented artists working in this medium who could help to create an individual design. The reflective capabilities of glass, whether it is with natural light or artificial lights reflecting brilliantly off glass surfaces, create an ever-changing light show.

In the bathroom, glass is traditionally used for shower screens. Framed screens were made from 6 mm thick glass, while frameless screens were 10 mm thick. Popular today is kiln-formed textured glass, which can be used for straight or curved shower screens, vanity tops and splashbacks. Glass bricks are sometimes a good bathroom solution, too.

And if that's not enough, glass is also a very convenient material. One, you can see through it. Cupboards with glass doors show off their contents without you having to open door after cupboard door in search of that elusive ingredient. Two, glass doors on book shelves protect against harmful light rays which can harm precious tomes; it also prevents them gathering dust. Three, it is oh-so-easy to clean.

One last thing on glass: to avoid nasty accidents be sure you always use toughened or tempered glass for interior features.

Great ideas for glass

benchtops ➢ cupboard and shelving doors ➢ doors ➢ leadlight (see below) ➢ room/space dividers ➢ shelves shower screens ➢ vanity tops

Cleaning glassware

Dishwashers do a great job but they're not always the safest way to wash special or precious glassware. To hand wash glassware use hot soapy water, then rinse in hot clean water. Allow to drain in the draining rack. Put the glasses on a tea towel and leave to dry on a bench. They will be 'crystal' clean.

Leadlight

Now, here's a design solution you mightn't think about much, but it really is worth taking the time to investigate it. Most people regard leadlight windows as a thing of the past something you need to take into account when renovating Victorian or Edwardian homes or art deco homes built in the 1920s and 1930s. However, leadlight can be given a very contemporary look as well, and it has some great advantages. Imagine you have a beautiful bathroom, but the windows look straight out to the next-door neighbour's roof. There's no view; it's a real mess. Well, you could use frosted or rippled glasses, but you could also create a beautiful leadlight to do the job.

Leadlight design solutions are only governed by your or the artist's imagination. They can be crowded with vibrant colour, or colour can be used very sparingly. They can be traditional or overtly modern. They can be simple or complex. And the colours can be incredibly rich and pleasing to the eye, changing constantly with the movement of the sun or outdoor light.

There are lots of opportunities to use leadlight in the home. Leadlight can look great in those little out-of-the-way windows we often have in kitchens and bathrooms, and makes for stylish panels in front doors and cabinets.

Do-it-yourself leadlighting is not for the faint-hearted, but there are thousands of Australians who have started from scratch and achieved great results. A leadlighting course is a good way of approaching your first project. Courses are available as adult education classes almost everywhere and they are a great way to meet other people and have fun. Alternatively, you could commission a craftsperson to design and construct a custom-made piece. This is a more costly route, but commissioning an artist can be a very rewarding process as well.

If you're a determined do-it-yourselfer, try starting with a simple project. This way you get a feel for the skills of the craft, and you'll most likely finish the project and achieve your aim which is a good result all round. Then you can choose whether to take the next step.

Leadlighting is a step-by-step process that requires careful planning and skills in glass cutting and soldering. Lead is very pliable, making it a great substance to work with, but make sure you wash your hands immediately after working with it as it's a cumulative poison. Leadlighting needs some special tools as well, making the idea of a class, where the tools are normally supplied, even more attractive. Leadlighting doesn't deserve to die out; it can enhance the modern home considerably.

Granite

The beautiful greys, reds, greens, blues and charcoal hues of granite make it one of the most elegant of surfaces. But this is just one of its fabulous qualities; the list of good points goes on and on. A non-porous and extremely hard quarried stone, granite is impervious to heat, stains, acidic foods and liquids and is resistant to chips, scratches and marks of just about any kind — although it's a good idea to seal it just in case, as some types can get marked.

Granite is so tough, in fact, that it is virtually indestructible. Take care how you place Dad's Riedel crystal glass on it or the only remaining bottle of Grange Hermitage. Delicate and precious materials such as fine bone china and crystal, combined with gravity, can meet their demise on granite surfaces. Granite is heavy too, so if you choose it as a worktop surface make sure you've got plenty of strength in your base cupboards and shelves to hold it securely and safely. It's not a cheap option by any means but it may be worth it in the long run — only you can decide.

Granite is one of the easiest surfaces to clean. A damp cloth, household spray cleaner and you're done.

Laminates

These provide one of the most, if not the most, popular finishes for kitchen benches, worktops and shelves. Known in the old days by the major brand names Laminex and Formica, laminated surfaces have been available for decades. They are tried and true and, to top it off, they keep getting better with a wider range of colours and textures.

There are two types of laminates: a thin laminated strip adhered to a ridged board such as chipboard or plywood; and solid laminate that can be supplied with curved edges, eliminating the inevitable line at the edges of the older strip type.

Laminates have qualities that make them ideal for kitchen worktops and shelving. They are very resistant to stains, moderately resistant to heat, knocks and scratches, and can be cleaned with the wipe of a cloth. It is not a good idea, though, to use a laminated bench as a cutting board; it will soon deteriorate.

Laminates provide probably the most extensive decorating scope of any modern material.

Cleaning hints for laminates

- For everyday care, clean with soapy water or a spray-on household cleaner.
- Sometimes laminated surfaces may pick up stains such as red wine. Patience is a virtue in these cases and it's absolutely free. The stain will slowly disappear in the course of normal cleaning, which is better than rubbing with harsh cleaners and finding that you have actually damaged the surface.
- With some accidental spills such as beetroot, grape and berry juices, first-aid preparations, concentrated bleach, oven cleaners, dishwasher detergents and artificial dyes or hair colouring, prompt action is necessary. Wipe off immediately.
- For stubborn stains, try methylated spirits or two or three light rubs with a cream cleanser. As a last resort dab the stain with a diluted bleach mixture (one part bleach to eight parts water), leave 3 minutes then remove.
- A green solution for stubborn stains is lemon juice or baking soda.

Don'ts for laminates

- Don't place electrical appliances or pots straight from the oven or cooktop directly onto your laminated benchtop.
- Don't use scourers and abrasives — they will damage the surface.
- Don't use a laminated surface as a chopping board or cutting surface.
- Don't use waxes and polishes. They merely dull the natural shine.

Marble

See also the sections on 'Floors' on page 58 and 'Walls and ceilings' on page 94.

Marble makes the most elegant of work surfaces, from silky black through beautifully patterned greys to creams and reds to ochres. But marble is also a porous stone susceptible to stains from various foods and ingredients, especially citrus juices, sugar and alcohol, and therefore needs to be sealed both for kitchen and bathroom use. Marble is a great work surface though, especially if you like to make your own cakes, breads and pastas. Rolling out and kneading your dough on marble is a pretty sensuous experience.

As beautiful as marble is, it's worth taking into account the cost of slab marble when working out your redecorating budget — it's not cheap. There are ways around this though: marble 'veneers' are available and there are marble tiles. Another solution is to incorporate or inlay a piece of slab marble into a workbench made of another material altogether. Make sure it is well sealed so that it doesn't accumulate grime in the cracks.

Melamine

Melamine is a coating applied to chipboard as an inexpensive, easy care, simple but quite attractive low sheen finish. It is used mainly for cupboards and shelving in kitchens, bathrooms, laundries and bedrooms, and on furniture such as chests of drawers. In its heavy duty form it can also be used for low traffic desks and laundry benches where it can provide a bright, clean-looking surface. It's easy to clean too; just rub with a damp cloth and a little detergent or all-purpose household cleaner, then wipe again with a cloth dampened with water. (Don't use abrasive cleaners.)

Standard melamine is not especially hard wearing, making it unsuitable for the wear and tear required for a kitchen benchtop. It is much better to opt for a laminated benchtop in these situations, which is much harder wearing, stain resistant and comes in a huge range of colours.

My mum used to polish the 'silver' about once a year and I was always happy to help her. There's something quite magical and very satisfying about rubbing the metal and changing it from dull and discoloured to gleaming and bright.

Silver and pewter

Although stainless steel has taken over as the best and most serviceable cutlery, the family silver still holds pride of place in many homes and is often brought out for special dinners and special occasions. Silver is called an 'inactive' metal as it doesn't tarnish when it is in normal contact with the air, but it does when it comes in contact with substances such as sulphur and chloride salts. That's why, on silver cleaning days, we would always be told the dos and don'ts of silver: that it goes an ugly black colour when you dip a silver spoon in your boiled egg; that peas tarnish it; that if you leave salt in the silver salt dish it will become pitted; and that food acids such as vinegar and lemon juice also react with it.

Here's the list of those substances that silver doesn't like:

- adhesives
- citrus juices
- egg yolks
- flowers
- fruit
- peas
- perfumes
- perspiration
- sea air
- vinegar

Although it's a reasonably serviceable metal, silver needs special care when cleaning — especially plates and dishes made of Sheffield plate silver, which can be quite thin and all too easily rubbed away. Be careful, too, when buying proprietary cleaners to make sure you find the gentlest possible and that they are actually especially made for silver — many all-purpose metal cleaners are simply too harsh. The good thing about silver is that, often, the cheapest environmentally friendly homemade cleaners are the best. Here are some simple recipes:

- Make a paste of whiting and methylated spirits. Whiting is calcium carbonate, also known as precipitated chalk and generally available from hardware stores. Using a cloth, or very soft toothbrush for patterned surfaces, apply to the silver then polish off gently with a soft dry cloth. Wash in hot water then dry with another soft dry cloth.

- Potato water — water that has had potatoes boiled in it can be good for cleaning silver. Dampen a soft cloth with it and rub gently to clean the silver.
- Make a pasty polish using half a cup of soap flakes, half a cup of whiting and a dessertspoon of ammonia in a bowl. Pour in one cup of boiling water and stir until dissolved. Allow to cool and store in a glass container. To use, shake well, rub gently on the silver then wash off with warm water and dry.
- Place a sheet of aluminium foil in a plastic bowl or bucket. A glass bowl works fine too. Place the silver on the foil. Mix a tablespoon of bicarbonate of soda (or salt) with sufficient boiling water to cover and pour over the silver and foil. Leave for ten minutes then rinse and dry. The trick is that the silver must be in contact with the aluminium foil and be completely covered by the water.

Take care to always use a soft cloth when cleaning silver and make sure not to use abrasive brushes, cleaning cloths and polishes. If you're a real perfectionist, wear cotton gloves (available from chemists) so that your perspiration doesn't retarnish the silver when you've gone to all that trouble of cleaning it.

Pewter

Pewter is easy. Most people like its soft, dull, slightly tarnished look, so the trick is not to polish it at all, just dust it. When you've done a hard day's work around the home and had beer in your favourite pewter mug, give it a rinse in warm water and a mild detergent and dry. If the mug becomes corroded, rub on a paste of flour, vinegar and salt, leave for 1 hour and polish off. Rinse in water and dry.

Stainless steel

After laminates, it could be said that stainless steel has created a revolution in kitchen design. With many appliances such as cooktops, ovens and dishwashers now made of stainless steel, in addition to sinks, benchtops, splashbacks, cutlery, numerous kitchen implements and pots and pans, stainless steel has become a very popular finish in the modern kitchen.

What a wonderful material it is — tough, long wearing, good looking, relatively easy to clean — stainless steel brings a professional look to the contemporary kitchen. It comes in a number of finishes, including matt, polished, patterned and sand blasted. The seamlessness of stainless steel benchtops and splashbacks can give an incredibly sleek look.

Stainless steel is susceptible to scratches and some corrosive kitchen substances such as acids and salt, but after a while these blemishes all just add to the look. Here are some tips for keeping your stainless steel in good condition.

- Stainless steel pots and pans are very simply cleaned in hot water and detergent or in the dishwasher.
- For benchtops, splashbacks, appliances and furniture, simple spray and wipe household cleaners and cream cleansers are very effective. Dry and polish with a soft dry cloth to give a lustrous finish. Take care not to use abrasives; they can leave scratch marks.
- Tarnished and pitted pots and pans: there are many proprietary products on the market that will bring them back to new. Make sure you use products specific for your needs.
- A homemade cleaner: try a polish made of half a cup of soap flakes, a quarter cup of whiting, 2 tablespoons of household ammonia and 2 tablespoons of water. Combine the ingredients in a jar or bowl. Dissolve well. Rub firmly onto the stainless steel with a soft cloth. Polish off, rinse in clean water and dry.

Steel and steel mesh

Steel mesh can be a great design and storage solution. Try it as a centrepiece on kitchen cupboard doors. It has the advantage of allowing air to circulate, which can be a great plus in tropical climates and can work well in temperate ones as well.

Steel mesh can make fabulous modern-looking racks and shelves which, if you know someone who can weld and you're a bit of a do-it-yourselfer, can be a cost effective and very chic design solution.

Timber

Timber makes one of the most stylish and evocative finishes for benchtops, shelving and cupboards. There are all sorts of timber colours to chose from to complement the atmosphere — both light and subtle.

Benchtops

With the great polyurethane finishes available today, softwoods, such as pines, can make excellent benchtops, the polyurethane sealing the surface against moisture and stains and giving it reasonable protection against heat. Timber benchtops, however, are really the domain of the hardwoods, which offer great toughness and strength in a heavy duty area like the kitchen. Although available in sheet and veneered form, the best solution for kitchen benches is solid timber. Another option is commonly known as 'butcher's block', which looks just like your butcher's chopping block. It is made of small blocks of timber cut across the grain so the end of the grain is the surface. It is a pretty good solution and can make a great showpiece, especially as an 'island' preparation bench.

Building a timber benchtop can be a big job for the average do-it-yourselfer, so it is probably advisable to have a cabinetmaker or kitchen contractor do the job for you, especially if you are also building cupboards underneath. Make sure you do your research on the best timbers as you will find some of them are not as suitable as others.

It's important that your timber is properly seasoned and it's a good idea to have the timber at home for a couple of months prior to installation so it can acclimatise to your home environment. Air-conditioners and central heating, which dry out the air, or a warm humid climate can cause movement in the timber resulting in 'buckling' or shrinkage in the bench. With some acclimatisation, the bench shouldn't be subject to expansion shrinkage.

Some timbers can be simply waxed and polished but, really, for hard-wear situations like kitchen benches it should be sealed.

Good timbers for kitchen benchtops

TIMBER	QUALITIES
Blackbutt	Western Australian hardwood, pale yellowish brown, interlocked grain.
Mountain ash (Tasmanian oak)	Pale pink and pale straw-coloured hardwood from Victoria and Tasmania, straight grain.
Pine	Pale yellow-honey-brown softwood, easy to work.
Queensland ash	Yellowish brown hardwood from the rainforests of northern Queensland.
Red box	Rich red-brown hardwood, wavy grain, some knots.
Blue gum	Common east coast hardwood, dark pink to red brown, easy to work.
Tasmanian blackwood	Golden brown hardwood often with darker bands, straight or sometimes wavy grain.

Sealing timber benchtops and shelves with polyurethane

Polyurethane is a 'plastic' clear finish that seals timber surfaces against moisture stains and protects it against heat. It is available in gloss, semi-gloss and matt; and with the addition of various natural timber stains and colours you can stain or colour your timber at the same time as sealing it. The following is a general method of application, but read the specific directions that accompany the product.

- Make sure the surface has been finely sanded in the direction of the grain (so there are no scratches) and is free of grease. Wipe with a clean soft cloth to remove any dust and grit.
- Apply the polyurethane with a brush in the direction of the grain, making sure that it covers the entire surface evenly. The finish will soak into the grain and any small blemishes, sealing and protecting them. Take care not to apply too much, or too little for that matter.
- Allow to dry as per the directions on the can — usually overnight or 24 hours — then resand the surface with a very light paper using a continuous belt sander or a flat sanding block.
- Clean the surface of all dust and grit and apply another coat of polyurethane. Repeat the process until the desired finish is achieved. For heavy duty surfaces such as kitchen benchtops, a third or fourth coat may be required.

Sealing timber benchtops and shelves with Scandinavian oil

Scandinavian oil, sometimes known as Danish oil, gets its name from its original use, that is, on Scandinavian furniture. The oil is synthetic, has a polyurethane base and penetrates deep down into the timber surface. It has a great low-sheen appearance and protects the surface against moisture and grease. As with all products that you use, apply according to the directions. Here is a general method of application:

- After finely sanding in the direction of the grain, ensure the surface is free of grease and wipe with a lint-free cloth to remove any dust and grit.
- Apply the Scandinavian oil with a brush liberally across the entire surface and leave for a few minutes.
- When about half of the area looks as though it has soaked in, rub the remaining oil across the surface using a lint-free cloth.
- When it is dry — note the directions on the product — rub the surface with a very fine abrasive paper or fine steel wool. Make sure you work in the direction of the grain.
- Brush in a second coat as for the first, working along the grain.
- Sand very lightly to finish and recoat if necessary.

Veneer

Although cupboards have been built for centuries from solid timber, both hardwoods and softwoods, these days it is worth considering veneered and melamine chipboard as a quality alternative. It has a number of advantages.

Chipboard is very stable and seldom 'moves' due to climate changes within the home such as extended periods of humidity or dry heat caused by central heating. It gives you a fantastic number of veneer options — timber finishes that would be very difficult to obtain in the solid form. Using veneers is much kinder on our forest resources than using solid timber. Also veneered chipboard is very cost effective.

Veneer or melamine chipboard, constructed in a simple box format or a series of boxes, is the usual method of construction for kitchen, bathroom and laundry storage. The base 'boxes' can either be finished in melamine or the desired timber with veneered doors and drawers sitting flush, giving a complete timber look to the unit.

Although solid timber shelving looks and feels great, the overwhelming majority of shelving these days is made from veneered timber. The same qualities apply to veneered timber for shelves as they do to cupboards and storage units, and the look can be every bit as good. The thing to remember with shelves is to take into account the weight they will have to carry compared to the span of the shelf. Most of us tend to make unsupported shelves a little too wide without sufficient support — and this is where solid timber can be the better solution.

Index

Acknowledgments

The publishers would like to thank the following individuals and companies for their assistance with this book: McGrath Partners, The Carpet Institute of Australia Limited, Jackie Warren, Jennifer Soo, Nicolle Adrichem, Liz Seymour, Cameron Hazlehurst.

Local builder and product organisations can be extremely helpful in guiding your choice of home products and their care. We found those listed below very helpful:
Australian Paint Manufacturers Federation; The Carpet Institute of Australia Limited; Paint manufacturers: Dulux Paints Australia, Porters Paints, Wattyl and Taubmans, Timber Development Association (NSW) Ltd; Sydney Building Information Centre; Building Development Display Centre, East Melbourne; Canberra Building Information Centre; Home & Building Display Centre, Springwood, Queensland; Home Base Expo, Subiaco, WA.